THE OFFICE AND WORK OF A READER

The Office and Work of a Reader

by

ROBERT MARTINEAU

Former Bishop of Blackburn

MOWBRAY
LONDON & OXFORD

First published in 1970.
Revised edition published 1980 by
A. R. Mowbray & Co. Ltd.
Saint Thomas House,
Becket Street,
Oxford OX1 1SJ

Reprinted 1982

ISBN 0 264 66576 7

Printed in Great Britain by
Biddles Ltd, Guildford, Surrey

CONTENTS

FOREWORD

THIS book meets a real need. The fact that its first edition has sold out shows that. And life for Readers has not stood still, for the second edition contains much new material. This book will be found invaluable not only for Readers themselves—in 1977 there were 6,526 Readers licensed in the Provinces of Canterbury and York, and 343 new Readers were admitted that year—but most clergy also would benefit from reading it. I am too often told by Readers that their role and functions are not always fully understood by the Church.

I can imagine no one better than Bishop Robert Martineau to write and to revise this book. Himself a former Reader, he has been a Warden of Readers in two Dioceses, and he was my predecessor as Chairman of the Central Readers Board, now become the Central Readers Conference and the ACCM Readers Committee.

Here will be found clear and helpful chapters on the functions of a Reader, such as preaching and the conduct of services. Also included is a valuable account of how the office of Reader evolved in our Church, together with a survey about Readers in other Anglican Provinces and an account of the work of Methodist Lay Preachers.

I think that the chapters on the Reader at Prayer and the Reader at his books will be particularly valued, and especially the chapter on Personal Relationships, which is a fund of sanctified common sense and Christian wisdom.

It is always interesting to compare the second edition of a book with the first, to see what changes have been introduced.

Naturally the chapter with the most fresh material is that on Training, for a new and more flexible method of training has been introduced for diocesan use. I see that this new edition also mentions the recent extension of Readers' duties, which may now officially include the taking of funerals, and which may also extend to pastoral functions in a parish, to which increasing attention during training is now being given in many dioceses.

The debate about the forms that the total ministry of the Church should take was going on before the first edition was published in 1970. My guess, is that it will still be going on when the third and fourth editions are published. Meanwhile Readers—the only officially authorized lay ministry in the Church of England—will continue to carry out their valuable functions; and this book will continue to make an important contribution to the ongoing debate.

✠HUGH BIRMINGHAM
Chairman
Central Readers Conference, and
ACCM Readers Committee

St. Bartholomew's Day, 1979

PREFACE

In approximately one-third of the parishes of England on an ordinary Sunday, a worshipper is likely to see and hear a reader; he would almost certainly be described by the worshipper as a lay reader. He may be reading a lesson, or he may be taking the whole service of Evensong and preaching the sermon. Apart from the fact that he wears a collar and tie and that the scarf over his cassock and surplice is blue, he looks like a clergyman. He is, none the less, very much a layman. He may be a schoolmaster or a shipping clerk, a labourer or the Lord-Lieutenant of a county, a prison governor or a plumber, a university professor or a bricklayer. All these are among those licensed as readers. Each holds a licence from the bishop for his work and was admitted to his office by the bishop. In 1966 there was a great Service of Thanksgiving in St Paul's Cathedral, London, to thank God for the restoring of the Office of Reader in the Church of England one hundred years before and for the witness and work of readers during that hundred years. Almost everywhere in the Anglican Communion, readers are to be found fulfilling this office. The details of their commission vary from province to province in the Church, but the basic work is the same. The purpose of this book is to see what that work is, what qualities are looked for in those who are to be admitted and licensed to the office of reader, and to make some suggestions to readers to help them in their work.

The ideas expressed have accumulated over a long period of years from 1935, when I was given permission to officiate as a reader in the parish of Aston, Birmingham. Since that time I have had the privilege to work with readers as a vicar and as a deanery chaplain, and as warden successively in Liverpool and Ely. Many of the suggestions made in this book have formed part of talks given to readers in those dioceses and also at the Conference for Readers at Lee Abbey. In 1970, I was invited to be the Chairman of the Central Readers Board and was able to have some part in the negotiations which led to the formation of the Readers' Committee of A.C.C.M. and the Readers' Conference.

The material in Appendices 1 and 2 to this book has been largely revised and I am indebted to many people for up-to-date information about the use of readers in other Provinces of the Anglican Communion. Among them I would especially thank the Archbishop of Armagh, the Bishops of Glasgow, Monmouth, Bloemfontein, Mashonaland, Hong Kong, Hokkaido, Fulham and Gibraltar; the Archbishop of the West Indies and the Archbishop of Brisbane; the Provincial Secretary in New Zealand, Tazmania, Kenya and Uganda; the General Secretary of the Synod of the Church of England in Australia; the Librarian of the Anglican Church in Canada; the Rev. John A. Schulz of ECUSA; the Bishop in Madras, Church of South India, and the Rev. Herbert Raynor of the Methodist Church. I am also indebted to the Rev. Robert Morgan for help with the Chapter on Training.

I

A Distinctive Lay Ministry

It is significant that just over a century ago, when the office of reader was revived in the Church of England, one of the principal reasons was to enable the laity to have a due share in the ministry of the Word. In the current debate on the future pattern of ministry, this factor must never be forgotten. At the present time there are also many other factors to be considered. There are less ordained men than a century ago, and a greater population. An appreciable number of those ordained today find a sense of vocation to a form of ministry other than parochial. The grouping of parishes in the country has been on a large scale, with the result that many country priests care for two or more places of worship. This grouping has up to now more than kept pace with the reduction of ordained men in parochial ministry, but before long there will be insufficient priests to serve the parishes as they are at present, unless there is either a considerable increase in the number of candidates for ordination or else the development of a supporting ministry of auxiliary priests. Other factors of quite different kinds enter into the present situation. In the last generation there has been a growing emphasis on the Holy Communion as the corporate offering of worship by the whole congregation within the Body of Christ. In an increasing number of parishes the Parish Communion is the principal and best-attended service, and Convocations have made regulations to enable lay people to take an increasing share in the conduct of the service, including the administration of the bread and wine. This change of emphasis has affected the work of the reader. In quite a different direction, the talk about Christian unity had led the Churches to study each other's ministries and to reconsider the value of those aspects of ministry which are different from their own. Thus a number of non-episcopal churches have reconsidered the office and work of a bishop as it is exercised in the Church of England, and the Church of England has reconsidered such offices as that of the lay elder in the Presbyterian Church and the local preacher in the Methodist Church. In addition, almost all the Churches (including the Roman Catholic Church) have been thinking again about the meaning of Diaconate and how the exercise of it should form part of the structure of ministry in the Church.

The debate about the emerging pattern of ministry concerns the sharing of the work and witness and government of the Church, or partnership in ministry. It relates to the balance of:

Personal oversight and shared responsibility
Whole-time ministers and part-time ministers
Local ministers and travelling ministers
Ordained ministers and lay ministers
Paid ministers and unpaid ministers
Parochial ministry and non-parochial ministry
A highly trained ministry and a ministry less-highly trained
The ministry of the Word and the ministry of the Sacraments
The service of the Church and the service of the world
A lifelong ministry and a temporary service
The diaconate as a step to the priesthood and a perpetual diaconate
The ministry of men and the ministry of women
The ministry of edification and the ministry of mission

In case there is any possible misunderstanding, these pairs of aspects of ministry are not alternatives nor are they contrasted in any way to suggest that either is superior or inferior to the other. Some ministers may find themselves sometimes in one group and sometimes in another. For example, an ordained clergyman may at one time be in the parochial ministry and at another be in a non-parochial ministry; he may spend part of his ministry in a way which is mainly concerned with edification and another part in which he is directly concerned with mission. A bishop is consecrated for the work of oversight, but a great deal of that oversight and of the making of decisions is shared with others. Again, the same person may exercise a ministry of Word and Sacrament; and the service of the Church and the service of the world are not opposites. The Church of England has committees and commissions studying and reporting on several of the aspects of ministry in the above list.

The remainder of this chapter looks at the office and work of a reader in respect of each of these pairs of aspects of ministry.

Personal oversight and shared responsibility

At first sight this may seem irrelevant to the office of reader, certainly if personal oversight is thought of in terms of the work of a bishop. The mood of the present, however, is to bring more people in to the sharing of responsibility and to see that lay people are given a proper share in decision-making. This is reflected in the legislation of the Church, especially in the consultation required under the Pastoral Measure of 1968 and in respect of the establishment of the General Synod and of diocesan and deanery synods. Readers do not have *ex officio* representation in these synods but, of course, there is nothing to prevent a reader from being elected; indeed, there are many readers who are prominent members of the General Synod. Within the last 5 years, the work of readers has come within the orbit of A.C.C.M. through the new Readers' Committee, so that the concerns of readers may be properly voiced at General Synod. In the Methodist Church, on the other hand, local preachers have a share in local administration of the church by virtue of their office, but for the administration at District or Conference level they have to be chosen for their qualities and their readiness to serve. In fact, a significant proportion of those persons elected for this work are local preachers, and there is no apparent reason why a similar pattern should not emerge in the Church of England. The licence given to a reader confers on him the privilege to preach the Gospel and not the right to rule the Church.

Although a reader is not given a share in the government of the Church by right of office, he is likely to be given the opportunity to share responsibility for parochial planning. This shared responsibility is the more likely to obtain in areas with a group or team ministry. In many ways the arrangements for services take on a form similar to that of a Methodist Circuit Plan. If the readers who serve where there is a team ministry regard themselves as ready to serve at any time in any of the churches in the area, they will in their turn be regarded as lay members of the team; sharing the work of preaching and taking services, they are likely to be asked to take a share in the planning of the work and worship of the churches in the area.

Whole-time and part-time ministers

As far as the reader is concerned, it may seem that here there is nothing to discuss. The reader earns his living one way and fulfils his office as reader in his 'spare' time. The number of stipendiary readers in the Church of England is so small, and reducing, that in the very near future there will be none at all. Even the number of former stipendiary readers supported by the Pension Fund is now rapidly declining. The whole-time reader is a relic of the past.

The debate on the ministry of the future, however, is not concerned with whole-time readers but with auxiliary priests. Although there is occasional lip-service given to the idea of a permanent or perpetual diaconate, all the development in the supporting ministry has been in the area of priests who earn their living in a secular occupation and who exercise their office as priests in a parish at weekends and in the evenings. Many of those who have offered themselves for this work have been readers, and their contribution to the life and witness of the Church has been correspondingly enriched.

In this whole discussion, both in print and in Committee, the ministry of the reader is considered mainly in terms of what he does in church buildings. One of the needs of the present is to see 'ministry' in a wider sense, and the reader's ministry provides an example which illustrates the point. For instance, there are about one hundred readers who are engaged in whole-time service for the welfare of the deaf. It would be hard to draw the line between their service 'as a reader' on Sundays in church and that as a welfare officer or as an interpreter at a Confirmation. They may not be stipendiary readers, but they are exercising a whole-time ministry. Once the idea of ministry is taken out of the confines of church services, it is possible to regard many other readers as involved in full-time ministry. Their ministry is sometimes an occupation to which they would not have been appointed had they been priests of the Church. For the very reason that they are lay persons, these men are able to fulfil their particular vocation and be engaged in whole-time service because of their Christian conviction. The world may not acknowledge their work as 'church work', but the Church should not dismiss it as 'worldly'.

Local and travelling ministers

This would seem the simplest distinction within the ministry, and with few exceptions the reader is a local minister. (The example quoted in the previous section concerning welfare officers for the deaf would be an exception.) The reader offers his service and is accepted for service where he is. He is without question or argument a parishioner somewhere. His services may be used on a wider scale but they begin where he is. The reader who is so occupied travelling to other churches that he no longer has a place of worship and centre of fellowship of his own to which he belongs, is putting his own spiritual life in danger and presenting a distorted image of the reader's ministry. With the development of groups of parishes, the reader may be attached to a group and travel within that group. If this situation obtains, it is but the Anglican counterpart to the Methodist circuit which is the locus of the local preacher.

Ordained and lay ministers

Within the whole discussion about the ministry of the future, this distinction is the crucial one. The fact that the Church of England now recognises and encourages an auxiliary priesthood, together with the actual fact that many priests are not in the parochial ministry but do not regard themselves any less as priests, raises the whole issue of the nature of ordination. This question cannot be answered in one paragraph in a book dealing with the ministry of readers. What is of immediate concern is the effect on the ministry of the reader, which is a lay ministry, of any substantial number of readers seeking ordination as auxiliary priests. In every diocese, there are a number of readers who are not only well trained and who keep up their reading, but who have gifts of leadership and a readiness to be of service and an understanding of the purpose of the Church. These men have just the qualities which a Selection Panel would look for in an auxiliary priest. Their ministrations as readers are welcomed by the people, who are ready to receive the cup from their hands at the Holy Communion. If they were ordained priest, their ministrations would be just as readily received. In every diocese also, there are readers of advancing years who seldom exercise their office. If they had been parochial clergymen, they would be in retirement and occasionally helping out; but there is no retirement age for readers. Diocesan Associations are glad to have these men as members and honour them for their service. The Readers' Committee of A.C.C.M. and Diocesan Associations will need to think out clearly the role of the reader if those with the greatest gifts of leadership are to be ordained as priests in a supporting ministry.

Paid or unpaid ministers

For all practical purposes, the ministry of readers in England is entirely voluntary and unpaid. The reports about readers in provinces of the Anglican Church overseas show that there are a number of paid officials who are not ordained and who either are readers or are treated as though they were readers. In some provinces they are given a different name, such as Catechist. There is a danger, which must just be accepted, that some people treat the unpaid worker as an amateur and the paid worker as a professional, and then attach to those descriptions the epithets 'second-class' and 'expert'. No play on words will of itself remove this danger, but there are many factors which help to reduce the danger. In many of the social services there are unpaid workers who are highly trained and whose skill is openly recognised; Marriage Guidance Counsellors and workers in the Citizens Advice Bureaux might be named as examples. On the other hand, the ordination of auxiliary priests in any large number may take away the idea of paid professionalism from the priesthood. In general I believe the Church of England values the voluntary nature of the service rendered by over six thousand readers and would wish it to continue.

Parochial and non-parochial ministers

Until recently the idea of vocation to the priesthood meant for most people a calling to be a parish priest, in spite of those exceptions who exercise their ministry as chaplains to schools, colleges, hospitals, prisons or the Armed Forces. These chaplains number nearly two thousand. They may not be parochial clergy, but the groups of people whom they serve are non-parochial communities in a place. There are just a few 'specialist' clergy who act as youth chaplains or stewardship advisers who are seen as helpers of the parish clergy. Priests who leave the parochial system and earn their living some other way, as schoolmasters or lecturers, were wrongly regarded as not quite exercising their priestly ministry to the full. This situation is now changing. The Church has a ministry to fulfil in every area of life and not just in geographical areas. Part of that ministry is priestly, aided by the ministry of word and witness. The financial structure of the Church of England is so bound up with the payment of parochial clergymen that it is unlikely that paid officers of the Church will be able to be deployed in any large numbers to work in areas other than geographical. This may be less serious than appears so long as there are Christian people who are ready to 'stand up and be counted' for their faith within a secular context. The opportunities for the reader, who by his employment and involvement is identified with others engaged in a secular situation, to bring Christian insights to bear on the process of decision-making are considerable. The fact that he is a layman, a person to whom things of earth have value in their own right, enables him to share the insights of those with whom he is involved in the world of things. The fact that he is a Christian layman, to whom things of earth have a value also beyond themselves, enables him to see every earthly situation and problem as having a bearing on the rule or kingship of God.

This ministry to an area of concern is not in opposition to the parochial or geographical ministry but is of a different kind. It does not consist of lunch-hour services, Bible-study groups and trying to persuade others to come to church. It is rather a ministry of infiltration through which the concerns of the world are subjected to the claims of the rule of unselfish love. It is a ministry of word, a ministry where what is said matters most; it is a ministry unconnected with any wish to boost a visible church organisation. It is a ministry for the lay person, though worker-priests may be able to share it. It is distinct from, and a counterpart of, the service of a man who continues in his secular occupation but is ordained priest to assist in a parochial situation in his non-working hours.

The degree of training

If the reader is regarded by the congregation as a stop-gap in necessity and as a substitute for the clergyman, then he would rightly be seen as a less highly trained product. The clergyman has had three years study at a theological college and is engaged for all his time on the job. The reader has studied in his spare evenings to take the General Readers' Certificate and does such reading as he can in his spare time. Of course there are clergymen whose libraries show when they last read a book, and there are readers who are academically in the first flight. These are exceptions to the general principle. The principle accepted by the Church as a whole is that the auxiliary priesthood is not in any way a second-class priesthood, and that any idea of a double standard is to be avoided.

The reader is not called to be a second-class priest but a first-class layman. He does a number of things in church buildings which a clergyman also does; for these he needs a thorough training, and the standards expected of a man to be admitted reader are going up rather than down. He needs continual refresher training on the job, and this is being professionally provided. The reader as a lay person, however, has skills and insights and understandings not normally shared by the clergyman. He has a calling not only to speak to the world, but to interpret the concerns and tensions of the world to the Church. Only part of the training for this can be given by the Church.

Ministry of Word and ministry of Sacrament

Because 'the Word was made flesh and dwelt among us' the ministry of the spoken word brings Christ to the hearts of men one way and the ministry of the broken bread brings him to the hearts of men another way. These ministries belong together. The dangers inherent in any system of 'mass priests' are obvious, but they can be exaggerated. The dangers inherent in a system of preachers who exercise no sacramental ministry seem to be minimised if not unrecognised. To perpetuate a way of thinking which divorces one ministry from the other is even greater. The ministry of the Sacraments is part of the priestly calling of the whole Church, the Body of Christ who gives himself to the faithful by these means, and whose presence among them is made real. The ministry of the Word is part of the mission of the whole Church, the Body of Christ who speaks to the world by this means, and whose presence as the Word of God among men is made real. Liturgical reform (not only in the Church of England) is making clearer the involvement of the whole Church in the action of the Sacrament. Participation rather than attendance is the part of the laity. The ordained priest (on behalf of the bishop) presides, certain lay persons take particular part in reading, intercession and bringing up bread and wine for the Sacrament; the whole confirmed laity offer themselves as the Body of Christ and receive in sacramental form the Body of Christ. Any lay Christian, let alone a reader, who thinks that he can fulfil his vocation and ministry without involvement in this priestly activity of the Church has an inadequate vision of his calling. The provision of sufficient persons in Holy Orders to preside at the celebrations of the Holy Communion is a consequential concern. The involvement of the whole Church in the ministry of Sacrament is primary.

Equally the whole people of God are involved in declaring the Word to the world. Those who exercise leadership in the Church must be able to explain to the world what is the purpose of its existence and the source of its life. The bishop and the priest should be preachers of the Word, but not they alone. All lay persons are called to the task of witness, not only by the quality of their lives but by their words. The influence of the spoken word in committee, among friends and in the home, is incalculable. Christian people are called to see the events of the world in the light of the Kingship of God and when they do speak, to speak accordingly. The authorised preaching of the Gospel in the context of the worship of the Church is a specialised form of speaking the Word, for which the reader is trained and licensed.

Serving the Church and serving the world

The training of a reader and those comments on his work in this book seem all concerned with his service to the Church. His licence states what he may do in the way of conducting services, preaching sermons and similar activities. This is inevitable; the bishop has no authority to give him a licence to be an official in a trades union or works committee. Readers do serve the Church, and they serve it very well.

If the life and activity of the Church were a withdrawal from the world, and the Christian's service of God regarded as possible only through disengagement from the world, then the work of a reader would be a waste of time. Service of the Church in such a case would be escapism. But if the life and activity of the Church inspire and equip Christian laymen to serve the world, if the fellowship within the Church challenges the world by its unselfishness and encourages the world by its joy, and if the Church in its worship declares the right attitude of the world to God, then service to the Church enables the Church better to serve the world.

Lifelong or temporary ministry

There has been much unnecessary confusion of thought in this regard stemming, presumably, from the indelible character which attaches to Holy Orders. Once a priest, always a priest, even if for any reason he is not allowed to exercise his ministry. Once baptised, always baptised, even if the baptised person no longer practises his religion or believes the faith. This does not apply to offices such as churchwarden; it is not true that once you are a churchwarden, you are always a churchwarden. In general the word 'Order' has been used in the Church to describe an indelible status, and for a task which may come to an end the word 'Office' has been used. The Convocations in 1866 recommended 'the constitution of a distinct office'. The rest of the Anglican Communion has largely but not consistently followed the lead of Canterbury and York. In Canada, each diocese has its own Canon on the work of readers. Canon 12 of the Diocese of Toronto begins 'The minor Order of Lay Readers shall comprise qualified laymen licensed by the Bishop.'

In practice, although the word 'Office' is used of readers, admission is not repeated. When admitted, the newly qualified reader is given two certificates; one is a Certificate of Admission, the other is the Bishop's Licence to exercise his office in the diocese. If the reader moves to another diocese, he returns his licence but retains his Certificate of Admission. He can then apply through the warden to the bishop of the diocese to which he has moved and ask for a licence to exercise his office. If this is granted, there is no re-admission to the office. There is a real sense therefore in which it may be said that 'once a reader, always a reader'.

Readers and deacons

'It appertaineth to the office of a Deacon . . . to assist the Priest in Divine Service, and specially when he ministereth the Holy Communion, and to help him in the distribution thereof . . . and to preach, if he be admitted thereto by the Bishop.' So the service for the Making of Deacons reads. The words could be reversed in the case of a reader. He is licensed to preach, and may assist in the distribution of the Holy Communion if he is given special permission. Given this permission there is little to distinguish the work done by deacon or reader. But the reader is a lay person who intends to remain a lay person; the deacon is 'The Reverend' and expects within a year to become a priest. The reader is permanently a reader; the diaconate is a stepping-stone to the priesthood.

The Paul Report (p. 156)[1] and the Report *A Supporting Ministry*[2] (p. 16) dismiss the idea of a permanent diaconate each in a few lines. The argument is simple, namely, that if readers are allowed to assist in the distribution of the bread and wine at the Holy

[1] L. Paul, *Deployment and Payment of the Clergy*, Church Information Office London, 1964).

[2] C.I.

Communion, there is no need for permanent deacons. If the need is for greater availability of the Holy Communion, then priests and not deacons are wanted. A few dioceses in the Protestant Episcopal Church in the U.S.A. do have permanent deacons, and in the diocese of California one of the archdeacons was a deacon belonging to the perpetual diaconate. At work as doctors, lawyers, officers in the Armed Forces, etc., these men were regarded as laymen; in the parochial context, they were colleagues in Holy Orders. The transition from one status to the other appeared entirely natural and seemed to present no difficulty whatever. The perpetual diaconate there is not a stepping-stone to the priesthood; it is clearly stated in the Canons of the Episcopal Church (Canon 34, Section 10 (a), (b) and (c)) that candidates shall not be less than thirty-two years of age, and shall have no intention of seeking advancement to the priesthood; if at a later date they desire to be advanced to the priesthood they must be treated in exactly the same way as all other candidates. These men assisted at the Liturgy on Sundays, took the reserved Sacrament to the sick and were treated by their rectors as ordained colleagues. Auxiliary priests would be able to do all that and more; readers with permission to deliver not only the cup but also the bread can do all that a perpetual deacon does, but are not ordained and are too often regarded as assistants rather than colleagues.

It was said by some in the Episcopal Church that the perpetual diaconate was revived to put meaning back into the word 'deacon'. Rather, it was an attempt to grasp what used to be signified by that word in the early Church and to translate it into modern terms. Those readers who are more concerned about service than status appear to be fulfilling precisely the same role with a different name and will gladly continue to do so while the debate about the meaning of diaconate continues.

Ministry of women and men

The question of the ordination of women to the priesthood and that of the relative status of deacons and deaconesses is outside the province of this book. Women may now share in the ministry of readers in England and, as is shown in Appendix 1, in most of the provinces overseas. With the increase in mobility, the pressure for some form of uniformity is bound to increase between the provinces. At present, the permission for women to be admitted as readers in England is so recent that to say anything about its effect would be conjecture. With special permission they may minister the chalice, and they may preach at the Holy Communion.

There is, then, no clear-cut distinction in the ministry between a paid, whole-time, highly trained, lifelong ministry of the sacraments and an amateur, part-time, less well-trained and temporary ministry of the word. There is, however, a lay character in the office and work of a reader (shared by some clergy) which both the reader and the laity of the Church do well to recognise. Apart from ecclesiastical laymen, whose service to the Church is both devoted and immense, the characteristic of a lay person is his essential involvement with the world. The word 'world' is used here in the sense of society organised apart from the thought of God. Using the categories of Yves Congar (*Lay People in the Church*, pp. 15–17)[1] a layman is one for whom the substance of things in themselves is real and interesting. As a member of the laity in the body of Christ, he also relates things to God and seeks to see all things so related, which is what distinguishes him from the secularist. The cleric, in Congar's category, is a man who so seeks to see all things in their relation to God that things cease to be interesting in themselves. The danger of clericalism, in that sense, is a loss of a full respect for things and persons in themselves.

The role of the reader, who is a layman exercising a teaching and preaching office in the Church, is of the utmost importance. He can interpret to the clergy what is happening in the world of

[1] Geoffrey Chapman (London 1959).

things, and he can speak to his fellow laymen about the relation of that world of things to their Creator, Redeemer and Sustainer. The priest and pastor is the servant of the laity in Christ; he is expected also to be the missioner of the Church to the world. He knows from his visiting much about human experience and he seeks so to enter into the joys and sorrows, fears and hopes, of his parishioners that he may convey to them that God knows and cares about them. A married clergyman shares many of these fears and hopes, domestic joys and parental cares. But the priest in general is not involved in the tensions of the world of things in the same way as a lay person. There are insights into a wage-dispute or a labour-relations problem which cannot wholly be understood by those who are not personally involved, and there are some insights which can better be understood by those who are not involved personally. The same principle applies in ethics, prison reform and in every department of human affairs. The ordained clergyman is withdrawn a little from some of the tensions and anxieties of the world of things so that by virtue of that detachment he may see the better how all things may be related to God. The lay person is involved in the world of things and by virtue of his sensitivity sees more clearly the value of things in themselves and their bearing on one another.

The mission of the Church is so to proclaim the sovereignty of the risen and ascended Christ that all things may be brought into subjection to God in him. This mission involves proclamation and worship, it involves Word and Sacrament, edification of the Body of Christ and confrontation with the world. The lay person, being a Church man and a man in the world, is at the point of confrontation. In general the ordained clergyman is not there, and when he is there, he is listened to by virtue of his involvement with the world at that point rather than because of his orders and theological training. The mission of the Church, therefore, is a task in which the layman is in the front line. Where conversation takes place, where decisions are made and where persons meet persons, there is the place for mission. The lay person, who by his involvement appreciates the values of things in themselves and persons in themselves, can speak and act so that they shall not be valued for themselves but for God.

This is the task of every layman. The parent in the home, the schoolmaster and the Director of Education, the shopkeeper and the magistrate, the surgeon and the nurse, indeed in every walk the layman can share in the mission of Christ. There have been and there are now movements of lay people who consciously direct their activity and thinking to this end. The Jocists, or Young Christian Worker movement, in France is one such in the Roman Catholic Church; the Parishfield Community at Detroit, Michigan, is a similar movement in the Episcopal Church in the United States. Christian Teamwork in this country has the same motive, and William Temple College acts as a centre of study and training with this among other things in mind. The Servants of Christ the King is a cell movement which seeks to bring into focus worldly and biblical insights, in the context of prayer and with the intention to act in the world. In all these and in many small groups of Christians which do not form part of any organised 'movement', there is a deliberate balance of involvement and of withdrawal, a balance between action and planning with prayer and study.

The importance of house-groups in the mission of the Church cannot be exaggerated. They do not exist in order to bring more people into the Church, but to send better Christians into the world. The role of the parish priest in house-groups is that of trainer and organiser, of adviser and inspirer; it is for the parish priest to see that the house-group is in right relationship with all else that belongs to the life of the Church in the parish. The reader can play a vital part in this development of Church life. He is a lay person and so a member of the group; he has been trained and has a licence from the bishop, and so can take a measure of leadership which will be accepted. If readers recognise the value of house-groups and are ready to exercise part of their office by their leadership in them, and if the clergy are prepared to trust them, then there is an almost unlimited future for readers to share in equipping the Church for mission. It is, perhaps, significant to note that in the Methodist Church, the former 'class meeting' has given way largely to some form of house group. These small groups, particularly when they have a devoted and efficient lay leadership, are a vitally important part of any Methodist society at the present time. The relation between these groups and the former class meetings is described in some detail in Michael Skinner's *House Groups*.[1]

In the last hundred years, the ministry of readers has gradually been accepted in the Church by clergy and by congregations. Their status and their function have never been tidily defined, nor are the Canons and Regulations in every Province alike, let alone identical. The attitude of the clergy varies from suspicion of someone who might want to usurp his position to the warmest co-operation with a colleague. The attitude of congregations varies from a grudging acceptance of a substitute for a proper parson to a respect for a fellow layman whom the bishop has licensed for his service. The reader's work has too largely been confined to the church building, though his licence mentions many other things such as visiting the sick and teaching the young. A very few parishes allow lay people to share in Confirmation training and after-care, though this is a vital area for lay work and witness.

The reader is essentially a lay person, who has been willing to be trained for his work. If the standard of training is allowed to drop, so that the licensed reader is little different from any other layman in his knowledge and understanding of the implications of the faith, then there is little future for the readers' ministry. If the reader aspires to be as much like a parson as possible and regards his whole ministry as something to be fulfilled in a church building, he may be useful in the maintenance of the services of the Church but the really lay character of his ministry which is its glory will be lost. If after his training and admission, he continues

[1] Epworth Press and S.P.C.K. (London, 1969).

his studies so that he is as well equipped as he can be to understand and to communicate the faith, and at the same time takes a right pride in his status as a lay person and is ready to take his share of leadership in the front line of the Church's mission, he will indeed be a 'vessel meet for the Master's use'.

2

Growth and Development

ST PAUL speaks of there being differences of gifts and of ministrations, but one Spirit and one Lord (1 Cor. 12.4-5). Any organised body needs men and women to fulfil a wide variety of tasks. Some tasks are done within the organisation and some can be and are done for the benefit of the organisation by outsiders who need not be members of the body. For example, it is not necessary for heating engineers or organ builders to be Anglicans in order to receive a contract from a parish church or cathedral. Other tasks, however, are done in the name of the organised body. In such cases it is important to know that the person doing the work has authority to do it. This, of course, applies to almost any organised body. If one is given a receipt for money paid, it is good to know that it is signed by a person authorised to sign receipts. The wearing of uniform is one form of giving this information. Thus traffic wardens and judges, policemen and clergymen, wear uniform when on duty as a sign of their right to act in that capacity. Each has some authorisation from a higher officer, and each has needed to show some qualification to do his work.

The Church needs men and women with a wide variety of gifts to maintain its life and work and witness. There are needed those whose primary task is to declare the good news of God in Christ to those who have not heard it. Others are needed to explain the implications of the good news to those who have heard, and to explain how the lives of men and women who have responded in faith have been transformed. There are those who teach the young, others who lead the worship of the faithful and yet others who look after the buildings and property of the Church. Each is doing his work for Christ in his Church and each believes that he is called to do this particular work. This sense of calling, or vocation, is over and above any outward authorisation. For this reason, the occasion when the Church gives its commission to a man to perform certain duties or to stand in a certain relationship within it is also an occasion when the man offers himself together with his gifts in Christ's service. Clearly this happens in Ordination, but in different ways the Church gives its commission to others. Sometimes this is done by laying on of hands, which indicates not only a commission to fulfil a task but also the establishing of a relationship between the Church and the person. For other tasks the authority is given by handing over some sign or token; it may be a signed and sealed document, or a badge of office or something similar.

Sometimes it is fairly easy to know and to explain what the task is to which a person has been commissioned. A choirboy is given his surplice or a badge; his task is to sing in the choir. The Sunday School Superintendent has a definite task. If each man or woman had one task only, there would be few problems. In practice, both now and in the early Church, men and women have performed many tasks. For example, the parish priest of today preaches the Gospel, celebrates the Sacraments, bears responsibility (with others) for the church building and its contents, visits the sick, keeps the registers and so on. In a small parish he probably also orders the oil, supervises the Sunday School, chooses the hymns for services, arranges for graves to be dug and edits the parish magazine. Sometimes he complains, and others complain on his behalf, that he spends too much time doing things for which he was not ordained and that others ought to help him. This can easily lead to an image of the Church in which the clergyman's work is thought to be the real work of the Church and that the duty of others is to assist him. In the last generation this false image has been corrected in so far as co-operation in the worship of the Church is concerned, and greater sharing in the administration and government of the Church by the laity is taking place. In the early Church, such a sharing certainly took place in the ordering of its worship. In the offering of the Eucharist, many people had their particular role; the offering was the offering of the whole body, in which each member had his part. Bishops and deacons and sub-deacons and lectors and acolytes worked together to make the offering of the priestly body. One of the earliest descriptions comes from the *Apology* of Justin Martyr in the middle of the second century. In this he describes the role of each participant, and has a special word for the reader of the memoirs of the apostles and the writings of the prophets (*Apology* I, 67).

The qualification of a lector or reader was that he could read intelligently, at a time when not everyone was literate. The practice had its roots in the customs of the Jewish synagogue, as the story related in the fourth chapter of the Gospel according to St Luke makes clear. The reader would be expected to be able to find the chosen passage, to read it in Hebrew and probably to translate into Aramaic. In the synagogue, evidently, opportunity was given to expound the passage. In the Eucharist of the early Christian community, the lector or reader merely read either from the scriptures or from early Christian writings. Gradually the tasks undertaken in the Eucharist became more clearly defined and divided into two groups, which in very rough terms could be described as clerical and lay. On the one side bishop and deacon were clearly clerical; on the other side, a doorkeeper was clearly lay. In between the two were those whose position took some time to determine, and in particular there were those who are called readers, together with deaconesses and sub-deacons. Gradually the distinction was drawn between those who constituted 'Orders' and those who held 'Offices'. This distinction was not sufficient, and there grew up the division between 'Orders' and 'Minor Orders'. In early Christian writings, the demarcation lines are neither clear nor wholly consistent. Laying on of hands was, in general, accepted as ordination to a Holy Order; laymen received their right to share in the liturgy of the Body of Christ through their confirmation. Those laymen who held an office, but did not share in Holy Orders, were commissioned without any further laying-on of hands. In the *Apostolic Constitutions* (8.22) there is described the ordination of a reader with the imposition of hands; in the *Canons of Hippolytus* (7.48) admission to the office of reader is stated expressly to be without the laying-on of hands. Similarly the extent of the authority given to the reader to expound what he had read varied. In one place it is implied that the authority of the reader is limited to reading; in another, there is long discussion as to whether he can preach in the presence of the bishop. Any confusion that the worshipper of today may have as to the status of a reader, and such variations as exist within the provinces of our Church in respect of readers, are no greater than those which applied to the uncertain status of the reader in the early Church.

So far, the Office of reader has been described as an auxiliary ministry; the reader was one of many who shared in the offering of the Liturgy by the Church. He fulfilled his office when the local Church was gathered. He and the deacon spoke to the Church, rather than on behalf of the Church. There were, however, others whose task was on behalf of the Church to the world; they were called teachers and evangelists. Here again we find considerable variation in the permission given and the mode of appointment. In the New Testament, the words 'evangelists' and 'teachers' are used in a list of those who receive special gifts of the Holy Spirit for their work (Ephesians 4.11). In the *Church History* of Eusebius, we read of evangelists as occupying 'the first place among the successors of the apostles'. These men are scarcely laymen, for Eusebius continues 'Starting out upon long journeys they performed the office of evangelists, being filled with the desire to preach Christ to those who had not yet heard the word of faith, and to deliver to them the divine Gospels. And when they had laid the foundations of the faith in foreign places, they appointed others as pastors' (Eusebius, *Church History*, Book 3, chapter 37). In a rather different category, we read of catechists, among whom should be numbered Origen before he was ordained presbyter. His position was interesting. When he was only eighteen, he was entrusted by Demetrius 'who presided over the Church' (in Alexandria) with the oversight of the catechetical school. There he taught secular subjects, for we read that he found the 'teaching of grammatical science inconsistent with training in divine subjects' and so he gave up the secular side of teaching and confined himself to instruction in the faith. As a catechist he visited Jerusalem and was asked by the bishop to preach in his presence (*Church History*, Book 6, chapters 3 and 19). It was not till later that he was ordained presbyter. Perhaps there is some comparison with the permission given by the Bishop of Lincoln to doctors of theology in the University of Oxford to preach in that diocese, which in those days included the county of Huntingdon (*Report on Readers and Subdeacons*, 1904, second edition, p. 63). The bishop's lack of impartiality between the universities was due, presumably, to the fact that Oxford was at that time in the diocese of Lincoln. The permission, or rather licence, given by Pope Innocent II to St Francis of Assisi and his companions seems to envisage that the Friars would be evangelists. The licence given was not just personal but, with certain safeguards, belonged to the Order; it remained within the power of each bishop, however, to allow or forbid Friars to preach in churches in his diocese. It is clear also that after the time of the Reformation, in England, there were many laymen who had permission to preach and some of these were paid a stipend. At a time when the number of priests was insufficient to fill all the parishes, parishes were held in plurality and the priest deputed 'a deacon or else some sober, honest and grave layman who as a lector or Reader shall . . . read the order of service appointed' (Archbishop Parker, quoted in the *Report of the Commission on Readers*, 1904). The priest was responsible for the Sacraments of Holy Baptism and Holy Communion, and for marriages; but readers could 'bury the dead and purify women after childbirth'. It is clear, however, that the scope of the licence given by different bishops varied very considerably and in 1571 a Canon was introduced in Convocation which appears to end the office of reader in the Church of England.

In fact, it seems that many existing readers continued to exercise their office and had their licences renewed for several years; but it is equally clear that new licences were not given and that the office of reader gradually died out.

It was not until the Convocations of the Church of England were allowed to meet once more (Canterbury, 1854 and York, 1861) that serious talk took place leading to the reviving of the office of reader in the Church of England. The arguments used and the terms of the resolutions proposed in the debate, which extended over a period of ten years, were concerned with providing a specific role for laymen to exercise a ministry in the worship of the Church. There is, in fact, a contrast proposed between the new agency and the old order of reader which had been maintained in the sixteenth century to provide services in parishes where there was no ordained man available. The titles of the *Report* of 1859 and of the debate in the Convocations were 'lay agency' and 'lay co-operation'; the limited scope of the lay agent was to read lessons, say parts of Morning and Evening Prayer, say the Litany and visit the sick. The difference between the new lay agency and the former Order of Reader was pointed out and the new name 'lay reader' was suggested. A subtle compromise was reached when the Upper House of Canterbury agreed, in May 1866, to a form of licence for the 'Office of Reader'. The word 'order' is scrupulously avoided in the document, and 'reader' is used without the qualification 'lay'. The reader needed to be nominated by the incumbent of a parish, received a licence to exercise his office in that parish, and had to return his licence if he left the parish or for any other reason ceased to work regularly in that parish. No provision was made for public admission to the office, which was exercised by the granting of the bishop's licence. The licence ceased to be valid on a change of incumbent, but could be renewed at the request of the new incumbent. Thus it is clear that the office was created to enable laymen to share with the incumbent in the conduct of church services and in the work of the parish, such as visiting the sick.

Nearly twenty years later a new development took place. Resolutions passed by the Convocation of 1884 provided for the Admission of Readers to their office by the bishop who should give to each newly admitted reader a copy of the New Testament. Provision was made for some form of examination before Admission, by which the bishop should be satisfied concerning the candidate's knowledge of Scripture and soundness of faith. The reader had to make and sign a declaration that he was baptised and confirmed and accepted the doctrine of the Church of England as expressed in the Prayer Book. The scope of his licence was extended to include giving addresses in unconsecrated buildings, which reflects the needs of parishes at a time when 'mission churches' were being put up in so many industrial towns and cities.

Five years later, the Convocation of York passed Resolutions which provided for readers with a licence 'of a higher and more extended character than the licence now commonly granted'. Such readers could exercise their office in any parish to which they were invited; that is to say they were not limited only to service in one parish. Their licence, however, was dependent on the nomination of an incument and ceased to be valid on the death or removal of that incumbent. The licence did not envisage an unattached diocesan reader, though the name diocesan reader as distinct from parochial reader came into common use and is used (without need of explanation) in the Resolutions of Convocation 1904. These Resolutions are enlightening in that they expressly say that it 'is not desirable under present circumstances to restore the Order either of Readers or of sub-deacons as a minor Order in the Church of England'. The licence given to readers, however, was further extended to allow sermons to be delivered and services taken in consecrated buildings, at the same time requiring the same assent to the Thirty-nine Articles as required of the clergy. It is expressly stated that admission to the office shall be by delivery of the New Testament 'but without any imposition of hands'.

While this process of development was taking place in regard to the Office of Reader, parallel development was taking place in regard to evangelists. This was not least because of the founding of the Church Army in 1882, and the establishment of its college in London for the training of evangelists. The Office of Lay Evangelist was established by the Convocation of Canterbury in 1898. The form of admission of an evangelist, according to the Regulations of 1904, was to be identical to that of a reader; any difference of function was to be specified on the licence. One major difference was spelled out in Regulation 15: 'The Commission of an Evangelist or trained Reader may include all or any of the duties of a Parochial or, in some cases, of a Diocesan Reader; but the work of an Evangelist will be more that of a Mission Preacher than of a regular assistant to the clergy.' This whole paragraph is repeated word for word in the Regulations adopted by the Convocations in 1921. The phrase 'regular assistant to the clergy' sums up the intention, implicit and explicit, in the whole restoration and growth of the office of reader in the last century.

The growth of what is known as the 'Parish Communion' since about 1930 presented parochial clergy with a new need for which they wanted 'regular assistance' namely, assistance in the administration of the Communion. Since the matter was first raised in 1857, the Convocations of both Canterbury and York resisted the idea of sub-deacons or any form of permanent diaconate or 'lay deacons'. The proposal was revived in 1925, the Lower House of Canterbury requesting the Upper House to revive the office of sub-deacon. In fact, the Upper House adjourned the debate but resolved (Canterbury 1939 and York 1940) that 'additional duties which, in exceptional circumstances and by special authorisation from the bishop, may be assigned to a Reader are:

> To read the Epistle at the Holy Communion
> To administer the Cup at the Holy Communion.'

Permission was not given for the reader to give an address at the

Holy Communion, but this restriction has been removed by the Canon E4.2(b) of 1969. It is interesting to note that in the Report of the Archbishops' Commission on Canon Law (1947) not only was it proposed that the restriction be retained, but all the relevant sections are entitled 'of Lay Readers' (proposed Canon 91–94). The Canons of 1969 opened the Office of Reader not only to men but also to women, with no restriction placed on bishops from giving permission to readers who are women from preaching at the Holy Communion or administering the chalice and paten.

In 1978 the General Synod passed an amendment to Canon E4, which now allows a reader to officiate at the Burial of the Dead. This may seem a small extension of a reader's duties, but it is a significant step. It underlines the pastoral involvement of a reader. Some such involvement has always been mentioned in the reader's licence, such as visiting the sick, but the teaching role has usually been foremost. Now the pattern is changing. Dioceses, and therefore parishes, are taking the pastoral role of the reader more seriously and the pattern of local training is being adapted to meet the new situation. As will be seen from the Appendix on the use of readers in other Provinces of the Anglican Communion, the amending of Canon E4 is in line with the practice of these provinces.

During the last hundred years, therefore, official documents regarding the Office of Reader have steadily increased the scope of the work which can be done by a reader. The reader is meant to be a regular assistant to the clergy, and not a substitute for the clergyman; the most recent extensions of the scope of his licence enable the reader to officiate at the Burial of the Dead, with the goodwill of the family concerned. In practice, the official documents very fairly represent what has actually been happening in the parishes in regard to readers. Permissions to do this or that have been given because there was a genuine demand that it should be done. The office was restored because there was a need for assistance to the clergy, and as much because a need was realised for laymen to share in the conduct of the worship of the Church. Since 1866, when the Office was restored in England, the number of Readers has grown to somewhat over 6,000. The dependence of the Church of England on their ministrations to maintain its present pattern of worship grows each year. The pattern of their activity is remarkably similar, if the dioceses of Ely and Liverpool are anything by which to judge, in rural areas or in a big city. On average in those two dioceses, a reader takes some part in a service three Sundays out of four and preaches on half the Sundays of the year; what is as significant is that two-thirds of their sermons are delivered within the parish to which they are licensed. This last fact is all the more significant in view of the fact that readers are used extensively when there is a vacancy in a parish. The parochial assistance given by the reader became recognised in many dioceses by the reader being *ex-officio* a member of the Parochial Church Council and, in some dioceses, of the Ruri-Decanal Conference. Unfortunately the new Regulations for Synodical Government of the Church do not provide the reader with any *ex-officio* right to share in the councils of the Church. The requests from the clergy that readers be given permission to assist with the administration at Holy Communion grow annually. It is an understandable sign of the times that whereas the requests used to be for assistance at the great Festivals of the Christian Year, now the requests are for assistance every Sunday. This is due not only to an increase in the number of communicants but also to a desire for involvement of laity in as much of the Holy Communion as possible; there has been a marked increase since the introduction of the 'Series Two' and 'Series Three' Holy Communion.

In a curious way, there has been a development in the Church of lay involvement in the conduct of worship quite apart from the reader movement, though not unconnected with it. The reader undergoes quite a long training for his work, he is formally admitted by the Bishop and is given his licence; he is dressed in cassock, surplice and blue scarf and his position is official and recognised. Is all this necessary for the reading of the Scriptures, or the conduct of Evensong, or the administration of the chalice? If the offering of worship is a shared activity of the whole Church, it is to be expected that there should be a demand for lay involvement without official licence. Putting it at its simplest, the lessons at Morning and Evening Prayer are read in many parishes by laymen (which includes women and children) quite apart from any Convocation Regulations. The Canons of 1969 (B12.4) do not restrict the reading of the Epistle and Gospel by laymen to licensed readers. The bishop may authorise a suitable layman to assist at the administration and to take the Reserved Sacrament to housebound sick persons. The Roman Catholic Church allows this also, since the publication of the Instruction 'Immensae Caritatis' in 1973. The demand from the clergy for this assistance has been insistent and growing. Until recent years, there were clergy who nominated a man for the office of reader and helped him through his training for the examinations solely in order that he might have assistance with the chalice. The progressive removal of these limitations of a layman's involvement in the conduct of worship is good. It is interesting that it has not apparently reduced the desire of laymen to be trained and admitted as readers, nor the desire of parish priests to have the services of a reader.

Note on the organisation of readers' work

The Resolutions and Regulations of Convocation from 1866 onwards made it clear that the ultimate control of the work of readers is in the hands of the Archbishops and Bishops. It is they who give readers their licence for their work and however the General Synod may extend or limit what may be done by a reader, the bishop of any diocese alone decides who shall hold his licence in that diocese and what evidence of fitness for the office he may require. In practice there is a large measure of uniformity. Diocesan Readers' Boards exist to co-ordinate the work in each diocese and the Readers' Committee of A.C.C.M. to co-ordinate that of readers in the Church of England as a whole. When the

Regulations relating to readers had been passed by the Convocations in 1905, a central body was established and a formal constitution of the Central Readers' Board was approved by the Archbishops and Bishops on the 21st November 1922. The Board existed 'to co-ordinate the organisation of readers in the dioceses, and to maintain and develop the work of readers generally, under the authority of the Archbishops and Bishops' (Regulations of Convocation 1939/40). The same Regulations ordered Diocesan Readers' Boards to be set up 'to raise the standard of qualifications, to supervise and regulate the work of readers and to secure due control of the organisation under the Bishop'. The Central Readers' Board which was set up consisted of over one hundred members; there were two representatives from each diocese in England and Wales, six representatives from the Church Assembly, together with co-opted members and others who represented Church Societies and Organisations in which readers worked. The present Central Readers' Conference has a similar constitution, but instead of the six members of General Synod 'such members of the Readers' Committee who are not already members of the Conference' have places on the Conference.

3
Training

BEFORE any person is admitted as a reader, there is a process of selection, training and testing. The selection procedure must take into account the needs of the Church and the sense of call by God to the person who is seeking to be trained as a reader. It must also take into account the ability of the candidate to undertake the training successfully. What cannot be described on paper is the way by which the call of God comes to a man or a woman which results in that person seeking to be trained.

When after much prayer a man feels that he has such a call, the first step to be taken is to talk it over at home. The present marital and domestic state of a man is part of the context in which God calls him to live out his Christian life and fulfil his Christian service. It is most unlikely to be God's will that a man should neglect his family responsibilities in order to 'serve the Church'. If he is married, he should first of all discuss with his wife how their shared discipleship of Christ would be affected by his becoming a reader. How would it affect their responsibility to the children and their ability to worship as a family? Such a discussion at home will help very greatly to test the reality of the sense of call. Motives in matters even of this importance are liable to be mixed. There is a sense of personal satisfaction, even of power, in leading the worship of God and in preaching in a church. Every candidate must examine his motives as honestly as possible. The next step is to go and see the vicar of the parish where he normally worships and tell him about the sense of call. The reader's ministry is an office and not an order; that is to say it relates primarily to a work which needs to be done, which is auxilliary to that of the whole-time ordained ministry. The approach of the candidate to the vicar. therefore, is to enquire whether his help would be welcome. It is an enquiry about the need for a reader and the opportunities of service, rather than a spiritual examination about a supposed sense of calling. Just occasionally, and all too seldom, the situation is reversed and it is the vicar who has spoken of the need and asked the candidate if he would be ready to be trained to supply that need. Whichever way the situation arises vicar and candidate must talk over the opportunities, the qualities which are looked for and the time which will be involved.

The third step varies slightly from diocese to diocese. Either the candidate or the vicar approaches either the Warden of Readers for the diocese or the (lay) secretary of the Diocesan Association of Readers. An application form will be sent to be completed by the candidate and his vicar; there will be a space giving the churchwardens the opportunities to state that the services of Mr So-and-So as a reader would be welcomed in the parish. Some diocesan forms ask for the rural dean to sign that he has interviewed the candidate and that as a result of this and of his knowledge of the parish concerned, he supports the application. By now there is some assurance not only that the candidate feels a sense of call but that there is also a need in the parish (and deanery) which the vicar and others feel could be met by the candidate's service as a reader. The application form is sent to the warden who will undoubtedly interview the candidate and explain the training procedure. In some dioceses, there is a chaplain for each deanery and preliminary selection is done on a deanery basis. In some others, there is a Selection Conference at which a number of candidates meet with a panel of selectors made up of the warden, a parish priest, a reader and one or two others. These meetings, together with talks about the work of a reader and opportunities for corporate prayer, last for a full day. The panel looks to see how becoming a reader would affect the man's life at home. in church and parish and at work.

When a candidate has been accepted for training, he is expected to undertake a course of study leading to the General Readers' Certificate. If a reader is to be licensed to preach in the Church, he must know what the faith of the Church is and on what authority it is based. He should know therefore enough about the Bible to be able to expound it and to read it privately to his own profit and publicly to the profit of others. He should know how the main doctrines of the Christian faith have been expressed and where some expressions of them have through their inadequacy led to errors in faith and practice. In other words, he will need to be tested as to his knowledge of the Bible and in matters of Christian doctrine. He should also know how God has acted in the affairs of men and how he is still acting; this calls for a study of history in general and of Church history in particular. He needs to know why the Church of England worships as it does, and the direction in which changes in that pattern of worship are moving; this calls for a knowledge of the Book of Common Prayer and its history, and of the principles underlying Christian worship. He must also study the history of the Office of Reader, so that he may exercise it properly when he comes to be admitted. Thus there will be practical training in leading worship and in preaching, and in such pastoral work as may be expected of a reader.

The purpose of the certificate is to provide the bishop with acceptable evidence that the candidate knows what the faith of the Church is and can communicate his knowledge in a form understood by others. The congregations of today have had a longer formal education than those of a generation or more ago and, as a result, the academic standard required of the preacher is greater than it used to be. The reader is proclaiming the same gospel in the same context to the same people as the ordained clergyman, and thus a similar standard of ability is required. However, candidates seeking to be readers come from a wide range of backgrounds and the course of training is correspondingly flexible. There is no longer a series of written tests taken under examination conditions, but an extended course of study undertaken with the help and guidance of one or more tutors in the diocese. It should be made clear also that obtaining the certificate does not carry with it the right to admission as a reader. Admission is entirely in the discretion of the bishop, who almost certainly would accept the advice of the warden; he might well give permission to officiate before the candidate has obtained his certificate.

The present system of training, completely revised in 1974, depends essentially on a group of tutors and assessors in each diocese. There are four main areas of study: (a) Biblical Foundations (b) The Christian Tradition (c) The Christian Present, and (d) The Work of a Reader. Some tutors are able to supervise all the areas of study covered by the syllabus; if so, a candidate is likely to remain with the same tutor throughout his period of training. Other tutors may be able, largely because of the time involved, to offer supervision for specified sections of the syllabus and in these cases the candidate may be under the guidance of two or more tutors before completing his training. The demands on the tutors are very considerable, but the system does involve far more members of the Church in the training of its lay ministry. This method also allows for the different pace at which candidates work, partly because of their individual background and partly because of the amount of time they can give to study in the light of their other commitments. In addition to the personal tutorial system, many dioceses arrange residential weekends for cororpate study and prayer.

The Section D of the syllabus, which relates to the practical aspects of the work of a reader, may well be supervised by the candidate's own vicar. Indeed, it is good that the local incumbent should be involved in the training to this extent; the partnership between vicar and reader is greatly strengthened if this happens. The Study Guide for this section describes four areas of concern, namely, Personal Prayer, Leading Worship, the Ministry of the Word, and Pastoral Ministry. To qualify for the General Readers' Certificate, the candidate must eventually submit four pieces of written work on this section (two sermons and two essays on practical aspects of a reader's work) to the Diocesan Assessor. If the Diocesan Assessor is satisfied with them, he will mark them and forward them to the Central Readers' Conference for final assessment. This system, which applies to each of the sections of the syllabus, helps to provide a common standard for all dioceses. This particular section, however, can scarcely be regarded as a subject to be examined; the most senior readers (and clergy) would be the first to acknowledge that they are learning all the time. The whole area of personal prayer is one in which we are all (hopefully) learners. The books suggested for reading reveal a pathway of prayer which may take a lifetime to travel. We can never say that we have mastered that subject. Thus this part of the syllabus may well be studied alongside the others and, though examined in a sense, be regarded as an area in which are are continually acquiring new insights and skills.

The section of the syllabus on Biblical Foundations is that which calls for the greatest study and the most reading of books. In addition to detailed knowledge of the Gospels and the other books of the New Testament, the course of study helps the candidate to see the importance of the Old Testament and the significance of the history of Israel. The misfortunes and hopes of the Hebrew people, their teaching about God's law and God's guidance of the nation's destiny, their way of worship and their idea of holiness all have their place in the understanding of the Gospel. This area of study, therefore, calls for a knowledge not only of what the Bible says but of the historical context in which its books were written; this is important in order to appreciate their relevance today. Our knowledge of Jesus Christ is so dependent on the Bible that the importance of this section for any Minister of the Word cannot be overstated.

However, it is not enough to know what the Bible says. In a generation when everything is questioned, the reader should also know what the Bible is and the character and purpose of many of its parts. Can it be trusted as reliable history and why are there sometimes differing accounts of the same incident? In an age when there are so many sects, the reader should know how books such as the Apocalypse or the Book of Daniel should be understood in relation to the Gospels or the Prophets. The course of study seeks to help the reader see the Bible as a whole, and to know what serious students and critics have been saying, especially in recent times. Otherwise he will tend to exercise his own 'criticism' of the Bible by reading and preaching only about those parts of it which mean most to himself or, alternatively, to attach an authority and attribute an importance to some parts of the Bible which others would not accept.

The sections called The Christian Tradition covers the history of the Church from the earliest days until the present time, including a study of the development of both doctrine and worship. The bringing together of these subjects, which used to be studied and examined separately, has been quite deliberate. They way the Church has viewed its own identity stems from its doctrine and will be expressed in its forms of worship. For example, what the Church believes about Regeneration will need to be expressed in its baptismal practice, and so determine the form of service used at Baptism and Confirmation. The Church of the present is the product of its past and the minister of the present must understand and value his heritage at the same time as he is aware of the mistakes of the past. The relations between the Church and the civil power, from the earliest days until recent times (and not only in our own country) provide a background for understanding the relations between the many parts of the now much-divided Church. Again, a knowledge of the history of the Prayer Book is essential for an understanding of the reasons for revision in our ways of worship today. The reader, when admitted and licensed, will spend much of his time preparing for and conducting public worship. If he understands the principles lying behind the forms of service, he can help the congregation where he serves to enter into corporate worship with meaning and to go from it with greater strength.

The last section, called The Christian Present, aims to help candidates see the relevance of the faith in the present-day world, what being a Christian in the world today involves. To some extent it covers many of the objections to, and criticisms of, both the Christian faith and the Christian Church. It seeks to understand something of the charismatic movement, for instance, and the relation of the Christian faith to other religions now practised in our own country. In addition, the whole subject of Ethics and of Christian behaviour in a permissive society is included in this section. Since the reader is involved in the tensions of the secular world in a way that the ordained minister is not, he can exercise his ministry with particular effect in this field. Indeed, though the tutor may guide and direct the study of the candidate, he is likely to learn much from him as well.

The syllabus suggests a large number of questions which can be discussed by a tutor and a candidate (or group of candidates) together, and on which he will ask the candidate to write an essay at home in his own time and with the help of any books on the subject. In due course, when several essays have been written the tutor in each section will choose and mark four pieces of work and send them to the Diocesan Assessor for comment. If in his turn the Diocesan Assessor is satisfied with the written work, he will send it on to the Central Readers' Conference for final marking; this final mark is recorded on the candidate's registration form. To complete the work for the General Readers' Certificate, therefore, some sixteen pieces of written work have to be submitted and approved. Candidates have very different academic backgrounds and also differing commitments on their time, but it would not be unreasonable to expect the whole course to take about three years to complete, allowing two evenings each week for study.

For a great many years the Central Readers' Board provided a correspondence course and tutorial help to any candidate in England or abroad. There were over two dozen tutors in its Tutorial Department and the course of preparation for the written examination in each of the four subjects (Introduction to the Bible, Church History, Christian Doctrine and Christian Worship) continued over a period of six months. In almost every diocese here at home, the tutorial network has replaced the former correspondence courses. But the Central Readers' Conference still provides a tutorial system with correspondence courses, which are used mostly by candidates in the Forces and by overseas dioceses.

The syllabus is designed in such a way that it can last a life-time, and is intended to start the candidate reading and thinking. Readers are expected to go on thinking and studying after admission as they did before gaining their Certificate. Indeed it is unlikely that any candidate will have covered more than a part of each section of the course by the time he is admitted. As an encouragement to those who feel able to continue serious study, there was established in 1933 the Archbishops' Diploma for Readers, with the approval of the Archbishops of Canterbury, York and Wales. The current pattern of work, which was introduced in 1974, requires candidates to submit three substantial essays on each of ten subjects, chosen from five groups in each of which they must pass in at least one subject. Successful candidates may apply for a Certificate, suitable for framing and signed by the Archbishop of Canterbury, and are entitled to use after their names the letters 'A.Dip.R'. The course is both rewarding and exacting, and the standard of work required is roughly equivalent to a university Diploma in theology.

Training to become a reader is not all a matter of book-work, and much of the training cannot be assessed by writing essays. The reader needs to read and speak clearly so that his conduct of services may be more helpful to the people. Almost everybody who reads in public needs guidance so that he can be heard, and the common faults of dropping the voice at the end of a sentence and of monotony both in pitch and speed can be corrected before they become a habit. Many of the duties of a reader can be undertaken by a candidate, or by any invited layman, so that it requires no special permission for a candidate to read the lessons at Morning and Evening Prayer. Subject to any general directions given by the bishop, a candidate may be invited to read the Epistle or Gospel at Holy Communion. Special permission would be needed for him to assist at the administration of the Holy Communion. He may also be invited to lead the Intercession at Holy Communion according to Series II or Series III or to lead the prayers after the Third Collect at Morning or Evening Prayer. In all these ways, the vicar can give the candidate opportunity to share in the leading of public worship and can advise him (and correct him if necessary) in this work. Some dioceses are adopting a system similar to that used in the Methodist Church, and expect a candidate to conduct services and to preach under supervision for the period between his acceptance as a candidate and his final admission as a reader.

4
Personal Relationships

One of the fundamental secrets in life as a whole is establishing right relationships, and any change in status involves adjustment in many directions in this matter of relationships. This applies to the child going to school, to the man or woman getting married, to anyone taking up a new job, and it applies to the reader who is called to a particular work in the Church. On being admitted to office, a reader finds a whole range of relationships which are new to him and others which need some adjustment. If he is to be at ease to do his work well, he must take these seriously.

When the Bishop admits a Reader to office, or gives him a licence when he moves into his diocese, a new relationship is established which might be summed up in the words authority and support. A reader is a man under authority, but he is also a man who can look to his bishop for support. A reader is an officer of the Church, and as soon as anyone accepts office anywhere he limits his freedom to some extent. For instance, a Cabinet Minister on accepting office limits his freedom to criticize the government publicly. He may criticize and argue with his colleagues within the Cabinet, but unless he agrees sufficiently with the policies accepted to support them openly, then he should resign. The more responsible the office held, in Church or State, the more the principle applies. There is no dishonesty or hypocrisy in this, since the honourable way of resignation is always open and can be, and sometimes is, taken both in Church and State. Now a reader holds his bishop's licence which gives him authority to preach as an officer of the Church, and to do a number of things officially.

The bishop is charged at his consecration 'with all faithful diligence, to banish and drive away all erroneous and strange doctrine contrary to God's Word; and both privately and openly to call upon and encourage others to the same'. He is responsible in the diocese to see that what is taught and preached is in fact the faith as held by the Church, as we understand it in the Church. The licence he gives to other people, clergy and readers alike, is authority to preach the faith as received and understood by the Church. As guardian of the faith in the diocese, therefore, there rests on him certain clear responsibilities. In the first place, a candidate desiring to be admitted and licensed as a reader should know what that faith is; it is the bishop's responsibility to satisfy himself that this is so. It is to this end that any training programme and examination system should be directed. In the second place, it is the bishop's responsibility to guide and correct those who hold his licence who preach something other than the faith; if the reader does not accept this guidance and advice, then it would be the bishop's responsibility to withdraw the licence given. The layman who holds no official position is free to express his own opinions, some of which may not be entirely orthodox. The licence to preach is authority to preach the faith and not one's own opinions; it is authority to proclaim the good news of man's salvation, the mighty acts of God in Christ, and their relevance today.

The bishop is also responsible for Church order, the relationships between different traditions within Christendom and between the embodiments of those traditions. By this I mean that it is the bishop who tries to hold together within the Church of England the varying strands of churchmanship and of theological emphasis, and to establish as much tolerance and harmony as possible among those who hold different but legitimate views. There are also all those delicate relations with other Christian denominations in which the bishop has the responsibility to act as guide and controller within the diocese, within the overall guidance given by the General Synod and the loyalty that he owes to his fellow-bishops. The reader, holding the bishop's licence, has a duty to keep in step with any policy officially given in the diocese. There may be times when in conscience he cannot take advantage of some permissions given by the bishop. There will be other times when the bishop does not give permission for something the reader would like to do; at this point, the holding of the bishop's licence calls for loyalty to the bishop's ruling. Only in this way is it possible for the growing together of the different denominations and traditions in the Church to be orderly and to proceed at a pace where not too many are racing ahead and not too many are left behind.

Particular examples of this arise when invitations come to preach in a church or chapel of some other denomination. Unless some general regulation in the diocese covers the particular instance, permission should be sought from the bishop after the goodwill of the incumbent of the parish in which the chapel is situated has first been obtained. The reader's own incumbent should also be asked, even in the case of a diocesan reader; much harm is done to the Church when a vicar has ground for saying he never sees Mr So-and-So because he is always away preaching at some chapel or other. The position becomes much more delicate when the question of Communion in another church arises. There is no written regulation to prevent an Anglican layman from so receiving Communion if his conscience permits, without reference to his vicar or bishop. A reader, however, holds an official position which limits his freedom to act without reference to others.

The bishop, however, does not stand only in a relationship of authority but also of support. If the reader shows loyalty and preaches the faith as received by the Church, he deserves the support of his bishop. He is part of a team, of which the bishop and clergy in the diocese are other parts. He has a right to expect advice if he should need it and the support of mutual prayer.

Some of the bishop's relations with the readers in a diocese will be delegated to the warden; the bishop will put into commission the day to day, and week to week, guidance of readers and their work. For instance, the whole matter of advising on examinations and preparation for them will normally be left in the hands of the warden. It will be the warden who will advise the bishop whether any particular candidate should be allowed exemption from certain examinations or should take some alternative testing. The general pastoral care of the readers, their fellowship after admission within study groups in deanery or archdeaconry, the holding of Quiet Days and so on will normally be the task of the warden. Dioceses differ in the way the use of readers is regulated, but the warden has general responsibility for seeing that no reader is used too much and that every reader has opportunity to exercise his office. Some of the administration the Warden may pass on to the secretary of the Diocesan Association. Whether at first hand or at second hand, the warden is the bishop's delegate. Every reader should not only know the warden, but should feel free to approach him at any time. The warden also has a responsibility to uphold the good name of the whole Readers' Association among the clergy and within the diocese as a whole. He should see that on occasions such as the Institution of an incumbent, the readers in a deanery receive invitation to be present and robe. He should see that no reader is out of pocket through having to travel to take services in another church, however much he may delegate the task. He will commend to his counterpart in another diocese any reader who moves his place of residence, so that he may be given opportunity to ask the bishop of the diocese to which he has moved for his licence. Similarly he will make enquiry of any reader who moves into the diocese and wishes to exercise his office and, if he is satisfied, commend his name to the bishop for licence. It will be the warden who, in the first instance, will try to sort out any minor causes of irritation which can arise between vicar and reader, or between a reader and the churchwardens of a parish he may have visited. The reader, then, stands in a relationship to the warden which is similar to the relationship between himself and the bishop. The warden can only do his work properly if the readers tell him what they are doing, the extent to which they are being used and any difficulties they experience.

A third relationship which is established when a reader is licensed is that between his vicar and himself. As this is essentially a very close relationship, it is essential for the well-being of both that it be a smooth and happy one. There are three main patterns of this relationship. In the first instance there is the vicar with whom a reader first starts his ministry; then there is his successor in the parish; finally there is the vicar of the parish into which a reader moves. As these patterns can be very different, it is good to look at each separately.

With few exceptions it will be the vicar of the parish who will have asked that the reader shall be given his licence. Doubtless the vicar and the would-be reader have discussed the matter for a long time, but in the last resort it is the vicar who asks the bishop to license Mr So-and-So, because he would be glad of his help in this way or that. The bishop looks to the warden to see that the candidate is adequately trained and understands what the work of a reader involves; he should also see that the vicar knows and understands what the work of a reader is, and is ready to give to the candidate all the help he will need, especially in the early days of exercising his office. Given this kind of understanding all round, the situation is really very simple. Vicar and reader form a close relationship as a team of which vicar, curates and readers are all members. The extent of the reader's share in the work of the staff of the parish needs to be spelt out between vicar and reader, otherwise a good initial relationship may degenerate; the vicar comes to treat the reader as a spare man doing certain odd jobs and filling in when there is an emergency, and the reader begins to wonder if he is really wanted at all. If the planning of services is done well in advance, with the part which each person will take clearly defined, the partnership between vicar and reader is more likely to be fruitful.

The reader has a right to expect guidance from his first vicar in regard to the way he carries out his duties. The sermons should be discussed, in respect of both matter and manner, in order that the word of God may be better preached. No one can learn to do his work better without criticism or comment, and the whole work of the reader will be helped if every part of it—his voice, the material of his occasional prayers, his reading of lessons and general manner in church—is open to kindly discussion between him and his vicar. In such matters action and reaction may be opposite but not always equal, yet there may be corresponding help to the vicar in his preaching, choice of prayers, reading of lessons and so on.

Between a reader and his first vicar, there is something wrong if a good relationship is not formed. Each wanted to work with the other and there should be little problem. In due course, however, either the vicar leaves and a new one arrives whose experience of readers elsewhere is different; or it may be that the reader leaves because of his daily work and finds himself in a parish where his services do not seem to be needed. Suppose it is the vicar who leaves, and that there is no assistant curate. The reader probably finds himself filling a larger role. The churchwardens are responsible for seeing that services are maintained and if relations up till now have been good they will most likely turn to the reader for more and more help. The people will begin to look on the reader as a kind of curate-in-charge who has not been ordained. If the vacancy is a long one, the reader begins to think of himself in this way; if he enjoys the work there is a part of him which will resent the coming of a new vicar. This is natural and not wicked; the alternative, which is a relief no longer to be so involved with this particular form of work for the Church, suggests that the reader is not as happy in his office as he should be. The new vicar is then appointed, perhaps without much consultation with the reader. He is instituted, and the bishop thanks everybody for what they have done during the vacancy; he has a special word of thanks for the reader. Quite unintentionally the impression is given to the reader that he is not wanted as much now that the new vicar has come; equally unintentionally, the impression is given to the vicar that the reader was filling in till he arrived and should now have a rest.

The people are so keen to welcome the new vicar that they pay far less attention to the reader, and he is quick to notice their coolness. The wardens are busy showing the new vicar all sorts of papers, and their dealings with the reader come to an abrupt end. Suddenly the reader finds himself taking second place and, to begin with, rather a lowly second place because the vicar is receiving extra attention because he is new. The reader begins to feel hurt because the impression is given, unintentionally, that his work did not count. Everywhere the phrase comes out 'Now that the new vicar has come . . . .'

Reader and vicar alike have the duty to recognise and act accordingly, with humility and with gentleness respectively. If they do not, the situation will promptly get worse. Not only will the reader resent the coming of the vicar, but the vicar will resent the existence of the reader. Quite wrongly it may be, but the vicar can easily look upon the reader as a rival especially if he has always been single-handed in the past. This will be aggravated every time the reader says 'We always do things this way'; or 'The last vicar always let me do this or that'. Such a reader represents the past regime and the former vicar; these have gone. The more closely the reader identifies himself with the past, the less keen the new vicar will be to want him to share in the shaping of the future. If the reader were a curate, the situation would be easy; he would go to the bishop and ask to be transferred to some other place. But the reader cannot move like that if his home and his work are settled.

There are three wrong things that he can do. The first is to sulk. The reader retires into his shell, grieved at the ingratitude of the parish. 'When there was no vicar, they were glad of my services; but now this man has come . . .'. The comparison with the elder brother in the parable is too close, even if the new vicar and the prodigal son have little in common. I would not mention this had I not had to try, as warden in two dioceses, to get readers to come out of their shell and to get their vicars to see their potential worth and to draw them gently back into a cheerful exercise of their work. (This, of course, does not only apply to vicars and readers; nor is it confined to the structures of the Church).

The second wrong thing the reader can do is to fight. Conscious of his status and of the privileges afforded him under the old regime, he determines to fight for the same status and privileges under the new. In order to achieve this end, he has to acquaint the vicar with what always used to happen; his attitude will be to demand that the same shall continue to happen. For instance, the reader has always read both lessons at Evensong and used to preach at least once a month; he always read the Epistle at Holy Communion, and so on. Privileges are seen as rights, and status in the Church looms larger than service to the Church. The reaction of the vicar may be exactly the opposite of what is intended, and he determines to put the reader firmly in his place. Sooner or later, one or both will come to the warden to say how obstinate the other is.

The third wrong thing a reader can do is to leave. Because his home remains the same, it means that he severs his connections with his own church; with a bit of luck he manages to get established in another. In extreme cases, the reader leaves the Church of England and joins some other communion where he will be better appreciated. This action has many bad consequences. It is, in fact, a form of sulking mixed with a sense of pride that there was not a fight; there is resentment and jealousy of the new vicar, who does not seem to appreciate all the reader has done in the past. It is a form of escapism, usually recognised by the congregation for what it is. It affects the reader's family, and their local church allegiance has to take second place to the reader's feelings. It makes good relations between the church the reader left and the church to which he went just a little more difficult to establish or maintain. Sooner or later it comes to the ears of the bishop or the warden, by which time the task of peace-making is pretty difficult.

Having described three wrong things the reader can do when a new vicar comes, what ought he to do? Is there a policy which guarantees success? Perhaps not, but there are some things which can be done which are more likely to lead to a successful relationship than others. First and foremost it is necessary to recognise the danger of being seen as a threat to the new vicar. The reader must be glad the new vicar has come, and must show that he is glad. He must recognise that the new vicar is in charge, and must be ready to be used or not to be used. There is meaning in the Methodist Covenant Service, where each person says to God '... Put me to what thou wilt, rank me with whom thou wilt; ... let me be employed for thee or laid aside for thee, exalted for thee or brought low for thee ...'. Let the reader be sure to give a special welcome to the new vicar, if possible in his home. Let him offer to help the vicar, by active participation or by standing aside, as the vicar sees best. If the reader is asked to do anything, let him say 'Thank you'. If the reader is not asked, or asked not, to take an active part in any service, let him be there in the congregation. If the vicar sees him as a regular worshipper faithful in his attendance at church, he will see him as a friend. If the vicar only sees the reader when he is asked to take some special part in a service, he is not seen so much as a friend but rather as a substitute and a service-taker. If the vicar does see the reader in this light and does not ask him to take any part in the services on ordinary Sundays, then he must not be too surprised on asking his reader to substitute for him when he goes on holiday to find that the reader has other plans already made.

The reader may find other opportunities to pour grace into an otherwise cold situation. Having established himself in his new vicar's eyes as a faithful worshipper, whether asked to robe or not, the reader should be conscientious in his attendance at any deanery occasions when readers are invited to be present and robe. However limited a reader's licence may be, and however restricted to one parish, he shares part of a wider ministry in the Church. When, therefore, there is a coming together of the Church on a basis wider than the parish the reader has opportunity to take his place in the wider fellowship and to be seen to belong to it.

If the new vicar is also present, he will see the reader in his place with other readers. In such a context there is no threat and no rivalry, but a shared ministry. If after this the reader is again seen to be faithfully in the congregation, he may find himself asked to share in ministry.

The new vicar, however, may be quite unused to readers and their work and may not realise how much it means to a reader to be allowed to share in the ministry of the Word. At this point the bishop, through his warden of readers, may be able to help. It may be possible for the warden to have a word in season with the new vicar, or to talk to the deanery chapter about the work of readers in general. This opens the door to both a danger and an opportunity. Suppose, when it becomes known that a reader is free to take services because his new vicar does not use him much, invitations begin to come in from neighbouring parishes. The danger is of accepting these without reference to the vicar. The reader may derive a sense of satisfaction that he is able to exercise the office to which he was licensed, and have a feeling that he is wanted. Rapidly, however, he becomes an absentee preacher. The effect on the new vicar will be that he is never in the parish anyway; this may be quite a wrong assessment of the situation, but it is likely to be the reaction caused. The danger, however, can be turned into an opportunity for good if the reader goes to his new vicar and says that he has received an invitation to assist at Little Puddlecombe on Sunday week and will it be quite all right if he goes. There is always the chance that the vicar may begin to realise the value of this particular ministry within the Church because a reader whom he was not using had the grace to ask his goodwill to be absent from his place in the congregation in order to lead the worship and preach the Word in another parish. If, of course, the neighbouring vicar rings up the new vicar to ask his permission to invite his reader, even more grace is added to the situation. In other words, the reader who receives a new vicar who does not use him as he is accustomed to be used, should do everything in his power to win the confidence of his vicar. Sulking, fighting or running away will do no good; only loyalty, humility and patience stand any chance of success.

If it is the reader who does the moving, the position is slightly different. Here, unless the reader promptly insists on being accepted on the parish staff uninvited, there is no threat to the incumbent. If the reader comes with his family and is as regular as he would have to be if he were asked to help at every service, the vicar sees him as a support not as a rival or threat. If the warden from the reader's former diocese writes to the vicar in the new diocese to commend the reader, the vicar will realise that this must be the man who has started to come with his family. Given this, the stage is set for fruitful co-operation. What the reader must not expect is that he deserves a licence as of right. A reader exercises his office because somebody wants him.

One relationship which is subtly altered when a reader is admitted is his relationship with his wife and family. Up to this point, husband and wife and family have sat together; now he is up in the chancel, while she is still with the family in the pew. The same applies to clergy and to choirmen and, in a different way, to choirboys. In a strange way it seems to apply more to a reader, unless he is very much a parochial reader. Clergy and choristers are less mobile over a short period than many readers, for readers are asked to go to churches other than their own to keep services going. Fortunately the use of readers to assist in their own home church is increasing. Some figures collected by the writer indicated that in the diocese of Ely two-thirds of the preaching done by readers was in their own home church. It still remains that one-third was done elsewhere; few clergymen preach in other churches to this extent. Even in the home church, the gap between chancel and pew remains. If the reader is asked to read the Epistle and to administer the chalice at Holy Communion, the gap is enlarged. However wrong it may be theologically there is an activity about ministering the chalice and a passivity about receiving Communion to which it takes time to adjust. For the sake of his wife and family, and for his own sake, a reader does well to make sure that they can all go together to Holy Communion from time to time and kneel together. For the same reason, a reader should watch carefully the extent to which he becomes a visiting preacher. Either he takes his wife and family with him and they all become spiritual nomads; or else he leaves them behind and one of the bonds within the family is loosened. Bishops understand this better than parish priests. The reader is very happy to receive outside requests to preach and help. There is nothing wrong in being glad that one's ministry is found helpful, but there is a limit to the amount a reader should be away from his home church.

In the reader's own parish, relationships need to be watched. The reader is at one and the same time a layman and a licensed preacher. In some ways he resembles a Warrant Officer; he eats in the Sergeants' Mess, but gets decorated with the DFC like an Officer and not the DFM like an airman. The reader is a layman, but decorated with a cassock and surplice and a blue scarf. In church he sits on the side of the clergy; in the Church Council or the Church Assembly, he sits with the laity. He has, as it were, a foot in each camp. It is most important that the delicate balance arising from this situation should not be upset, or allowed to cause upset to others. His work of preaching and reading is seen; it is visible to all the congregation. Therefore it is the lay role which needs to be more visible; otherwise, quite unintentionally and almost unconsciously, the impression will be given that the reader thinks himself too holy to roll his sleeves up. From time to time he should seek the occasion to join some working party in the parish to clean up the churchyard, or prepare the Harvest Supper, or act as timekeeper for the children's sports. He should be ready, if he is equipped and able, to represent the Church Council as Manager of the Church School or in some other capacity. The reader has an opportunity to bridge the gap between ministry to the congregation and the ministry of the congregation. If he confines his church activities to what he does when he is robed, he loses this opportunity to set forward this partnership in ministry.

He has a further opportunity. In a peculiar way he understands the feelings of both parson and people and can do much by interpreting each to the other. In some parochial church councils this could be invaluable!

Another relationship established when a reader is licensed is that with his fellow readers. In most dioceses the Service of Admission and Licensing of Readers is made an occasion when all the readers in the diocese are invited. In this way a reader is admitted not only to an office but to a fellowship. When an admission takes place in the parish church where a reader is to serve, this element is lacking. A reader's ministry will be poorer, and therefore his contribution to the work of God in his church will be less, if he holds aloof from the fellowship of other readers in the diocese and deanery. In his turn he will be able to help those who will be admitted and licensed in subsequent years to find fellowship in this ministry. If a study group is formed, he will have something to give and to learn. Clearly the warden must see that too many demands are not made on readers to attend meetings, and he should be wise enough to see when the law of diminishing returns begins to apply, but the warden should see that opportunity is given for readers to make real their fellowship and to derive benefit from it.

Finally the relations between a reader and the people with whom he works will be very slightly altered. Most people judge their neighbours silently, and many of a reader's fellow-workers will know that he is a reader. Let us hope that no reader would wish to conceal the fact as though he were ashamed of it. Most people are more vocal when they condemn than when they praise; they are usually quicker in reaching superficial judgements, and take longer to reach a judgement of anything that matters deeply. Thus the reader is probably unaware of the silent and almost unconscious judgement of the faith which is going on as his life and behaviour is watched. The clergyman will be differently judged by the world, for there is a sense in which he is withdrawn and is set over against the world. The reasons why a reader takes up his work in the Church will be less obvious, especially if he avoids the danger of becoming an imitation parson. People are unlikely to ask a reader why he has become one; they will just look and see. The image that many people have of the Church is of an institution separate from the world, whose life is irrelevant in the world of the twentieth century; they do not see the Church having any connection with such things as the Trade Union Movement or the Works Football Club or scientific enquiry or market research. Whatever the reader's everyday work and secular involvement, if he withdraws from it because he is now engaged in 'Church work', the image of the Church as withdrawn from and unconcerned with the world will only be strengthened.

5
Conduct of Services

A READER is likely to be asked, sometimes at short notice, to conduct Morning or Evening Prayer single-handed in church buildings with which he is unfamiliar. When taking part in such a service in one's own parish church, there are many things which can be taken for granted. In such a case, the reader knows where he will robe and whether the choir (if any) robes, and he is familiar with the normal procedure for coming in and going out. When asked to go to an unfamiliar church, it is good to find out in advance some general information. Is there a choir and is the service sung? Does anybody else take part, such as reading a lesson? Who chooses the psalms and hymns, and how many hymns are usually sung? What hymn-book is used? Is the service that of the Prayer Book or Series III? If the latter, what canticles are to be used?

Having collected as much basic knowledge as possible, the reader is wise to take a few practical precautions. He will arrive in time to have a good look round the vestry and chancel and to see where he will be sitting and how to get to the pulpit; he is wise to check the position of a light switch in the pulpit and the height of the reading desk there. In a very few churches, even getting to the pulpit can present a problem! He will check where the alms dish is placed and how it is taken out of church; clearly he does not want to arrive at the west door carrying it out, and have to hold it when saying good-night to the congregation. The wise reader will have a word with the organist before the service to find out whether the Creed, the Lord's Prayer and the Collects are normally said or sung; even such apparently small things as, for instance, whether the 'Let us pray' before the Lesser Litany is intoned standing or kneeling. These may seem very small matters, but they make a considerable difference to the smooth running of a service.

When we minister in this way in particular churches on isolated occasions, and also during a vacancy in a parish, courtesy and good sense demand that we should maintain the customs which exist there. It is true that there is a wide variety of use in the Church of England, but each congregation is familiar with its own way of doing things. It is not for the visiting reader or clergyman to change that use.

Having taken precautions to avoid as many of the common pitfalls as possible, the reader now prepares to conduct Matins or Evensong. His task is to lead an act of worship of Almighty God, and he approaches this task with the utmost reverence. Having put on his cassock, he will go into the chancel to pray that God will free him from undue self-consciousness; that the offering of worship in all its variety may be to God's glory; that the prayers, the reading of scripture, the psalms and hymns, and the sermon may be blessed and used by God to strengthen the faith of his people, to deepen their love of Christ and to equip them for his service. The very fact of seeing the reader praying before the service will help towards this end. Returning to the vestry to put on the rest of his robes, he joins the choir (if any) for the 'Vestry Prayer'. (It is not the responsibility of the visiting reader to control the choir, nor should he rebuke a chorister for being late. He may, if he feels very strongly, tell the organist how certain behaviour made the offering of worship more difficult; but he should only do so when the circumstances giving rise to the complaint are of a serious nature.) The 'Vestry Prayer' is the preparation of the choristers for the total act of worship and for their part in it; it is not a preface to the service for the congregation.

Every movement of the person conducting a service either helps or hinders the total act of worship. Unfortunately the hindrances are more obvious than the helps. To trip on a step, to drop one's notes in the aisle or any similar mishap distracts the attention of the congregation. The fact that such mishaps do not occur may not be consciously noticed; the care taken to see that they do not occur is none the less part of the offering of worship.

Very small things, like not cutting corners when entering the chancel or moving from prayer-desk to lectern, create an atmosphere of reverence; equally, an excess of fussiness can and does distract the people.

If there is an opening hymn, announce it clearly. If you must repeat the number, just repeat the number. Have you not heard of the clergyman who was asked which bus went to High Street and replied 'Bus number 23, the twenty-third bus'. Avoid clichés, and glimpses of what should be obvious, such as 'We will all sing together, to the glory of God, hymn number so-and-so'. The object of announcing the hymn number is to enable the congregation to find the right one; assuming there is a hymn-board clearly visible, one announcement should be sufficient.

When the hymn is over, allow sufficient pause for members of the congregation to put down their books and to be ready for the opening section of the service—Sentences and Exhortation, Confession and Prayer for Forgiveness. The opening Sentence should be clear and distinct. It declares the need for confession of sin or (as in some of the more recent alternatives) the message of the season. In the Exhortation the minister addresses the people, and he should, therefore, face those to whom he is speaking. Unless it has been discovered in advance that any alternative to the Exhortation in the Prayer Book is commonly used, the Prayer Book form should be used. This is not only a matter of good order but of good sense. The congregation have only their tradition and their Prayer Book to guide them, and if right at the outset of their act of worship an unfamiliar Exhortation is used, which is not in their Prayer Book, they will be both confused and annoyed.

The Reader then kneels for the General Confession, and allows sufficient time for the congregation to do the same before starting the prayer. It is not my concern to argue the merits or demerits of repeating the opening phrase of this or any other prayer said together. Unless we are in charge, on a fairly permanent basis, we ought to abide by the custom prevailing in the church where we go. Lead the prayer clearly at a steady pace (the larger the building, the slower the pace). Holding one's hands to the face distorts the sound; this applies even more strongly when versicles are sung.

The General Confession ended, the reader remains kneeling and reads the Collect for the 21st Sunday after Trinity: 'Grant, we beseech thee, merciful Lord, to thy faithful people pardon and peace, that they may be cleansed from all their sins, and serve thee with a quiet mind; through Jesus Christ our Lord.'

The Lord's Prayer follows at once, bearing in mind what is said above about repeating the opening words, or otherwise. Still kneeling, the reader sings 'O Lord, open thou our lips', having been given a note from the organ. (If you can't sing, don't, having had a word with the organist first; if you do there is likely to be someone musical in the congregation whose sole memory of the service will be that the reader couldn't sing.) Stand for the Gloria, and give everyone else time to stand before you sing it; during the pause, pick up your hymn-sheet so that you can announce the psalm number without further movement after 'The Lord's name be praised'.

When announcing the psalm, remember that the purpose is to enable the congregation to find the place. In places where there are Prayer-Books which have Roman numerals for the psalms, the congregation need help; if so, it may be useful to explain that Psalm 65 is the first psalm for the twelfth evening or (if there is a standard Prayer Book in all the pews) that it will be found on page so-and-so. To give an introduction to the psalm in one sentence makes a real difference to its intelligent singing, and to this end the brief introductions written by Bishop G. A. Chase as an appendix to *A Companion to the Revised Psalter*[1] are designed for this very purpose. If there are two psalms which are not consecutive or even nearly so, arrange beforehand with the organist to have a brief pause so that the second can be announced again briefly. It is not easy for the congregation to turn quickly from Psalm 19 to 85 (Christmas morning) or from 86 to 130

[1] S.P.C.K. (London, 1963).

(Palm Sunday evening); many members of the congregation will have forgotten what the second psalm number was.

The reading of the Lessons should have been prepared with as much diligence as the sermon. Here is God's word to his people, which we are privileged to read. A reader or a clergyman who uses the last few verses of the psalm looking at the Lectionary to see what the Lesson is to be reveals an unpreparedness which is culpable; this is not leadership in the worship of God. Let the Bible be already open at the right place and a marker placed where the second Lesson is to be found. Move at an even pace to the lectern, without cutting corners, and arrive in time for the Gloria which follows the psalm before the Lesson. Give time for the members of the congregation to sit and prepare themselves to listen, and then announce the Lesson clearly. The method of announcing approved in the *Alternative Services Measure*[1] is to be encouraged: 'The first lesson is taken from the book of the prophet Ezekiel, in the thirty-fourth chapter, beginning at the eleventh verse', or the more modern form '. . . from the book of the prophet Ezekiel, chapter thirty-four at verse eleven'. A few words of explanation of the reading can be very helpful, and there are several booklets of such Introductions to the Lessons. It is usually apparent from the way a Lesson is read whether the reader of it has prepared in advance. Let the reading be not too fast; indeed in a large church it may seem to the reader to be very slow, and the voice must not be dropped at the end of sentences. (The quickest way to learn how well or badly one reads a Lesson is to use a tape-recorder and then to sit near the back of the building and let the tape be played over again). At the end of the Lesson let there be a slight pause before saying 'Here ends the first Lesson'. In those churches where the congregation have been trained to have a minute or two of silence after the readings, the Lessons take on a quite new significance. If there is any doubt as to the correct name of a book of the Bible (e.g. Kings or The

[1] Prayer Book (Alternative and Other Services) Measure, p. 28, H.M.S.O. (London, 1965).

Kings; or the last book in the New Testament) the simple rule is to look at the beginning of the book itself and see the exact title given. These titles are slightly different in new translations, but the title used in the version which is being read is the title to announce.

Canticles are not normally announced unless alternatives are being used; if so, it does help the congregation if the fact is clearly announced and some guidance given as to where the canticle can be found. Such announcements slightly interrupt the smooth flow of a service, but less so than the silent interruption to the flow of thought when a worshipper does not know what is happening and takes his mind away from the worship of God to discover what he should be singing. The American churches have duplicated Bulletins each Sunday with all the details of the service set out, and the pages where each part is to be found; some English churches are adopting this practice.

After the second canticle, the Creed is said or sung. In this, and in all such matters, the practice of the church visited should be followed by those of who do the visiting. A reader or visiting minister who officiously turns east in a church where it is not the custom, or who stands rigidly looking north or south when the choir have turned to the east, is likely to cause offence to the Family of God; he is hurting the Body of Christ. For the salutation, 'The Lord be with you', the reader should look at the people whom he is addressing; he should face the congregation. This general principle applies on all occasions when the minister is speaking to the people; what must not be imagined, however, is that God is somewhere behind the altar. The versicles may be sung standing or kneeling, but the voice carries better if the reader is standing. Let the pace be natural and constant both in the versicles and in the Collects, if they are also sung. If there is more than one Collect as, for instance, during Lent or when a Saint's Day falls on a Sunday, be sure that both organist and choir know what is going to happen. The order in which they should be said or sung can be determined from one or other of the standard church calendars; such a calendar should be part of the equipment of every reader.

After the third Collect there is normally an anthem or a hymn. If it is a hymn there is no problem. Give the people time to rise from their knees and sit down, announce the hymn clearly facing the people and all is well. If an anthem is sung, turn to the people and tell them simply that the choir will sing the anthem 'O taste and see how gracious the Lord is'; the music is by Vaughan Williams. The temptation to join in, even if you know the anthem by heart, should be resisted. This is the choir's offering which they have rehearsed; besides, you can easily be caught out if it has been decided to repeat a part or omit some part!

The prayers after the third Collect should have been meticulously prepared. There are several good collections of suitable prayers and a reader should have one or two such books. If a diocese wants its readers to do their job well, it would be money well spent to provide all readers with a good book of such prayers. These prayers should follow a clear pattern and should not be a small service in themselves. Praise and penitence have already had their place in the Office which has just been offered to God; therefore they should not be repeated. On some occasions there may be good reason to offer thanksgiving for some particular blessing; on all occasions there is ground for giving thanks to God, and the General Thanksgiving is never out of place.

Intercessions should relate to the current needs of the world and to the concerns of the people. The people are members of many communities; the Church as a whole, the Anglican Church and diocese and parish in particular; their country, town and neighbourhood, and so on. These concerns form proper occasions for intercession at this point, and special needs, e.g. the peace of the world or the unity of the Church may be remembered. If there are topical troubles such as industrial unrest, flood, disaster etc. these may also rightly be mentioned. The sick in body and mind should be remembered, and a short pause given to enable individuals to think silently of some special sick person whom they know. There is something to be said for not concluding these prayers with the Grace, which can then be said at the end of the service.

The visiting reader will have found out in advance whether these occasional prayers are said from the reading desk or from the nave, and will abide by the prevailing custom. He will have markers in any book he is using, and it helps the congregation to share intelligently if the purpose of each prayer is stated. 'Let us pray for those made homeless because of the earthquake in Alaska', and so on. Four or five prayers, carefully chosen and clearly read, are sufficient. When a reader ministers regularly at the same church, it is possible sometimes to place the occasional prayers after the sermon. In this way the theme of the sermon can be taken up into the prayers. For example, if the sermon was on the theme of the healing power of God, there could be prayers for the healing of nations, the healing of the divisions in the Church, the healing of broken homes, and the healing of the sick. It is wise to explain carefully to any congregation why a change is being made in the order of the service to which it is accustomed.

Banns of marriage may need to be read after the occasional prayers, if they have not already been read during the Holy Communion earlier. If there are such banns to be read there are several points to watch. First, a good look at the banns book is needed to see how many are being read for the first, second or third times; second, make sure you can read all the names; third, be quite sure to sign each entry and see that the date of reading has been inserted. The form of words for publishing banns of marriage is set out in the Prayer Book (in the General Rubrics preceding the Marriage Service). 'I publish the banns of marriage between N of . . . and M of . . . If any of you know cause or just impediment why these two persons should not be joined together in Holy Matrimony, ye are to declare it. This is the first (second or third) time of asking.' If there are many sets of banns, read those which are being read for the third time and say 'This is the third time of asking'; then those for the second and first time. At the conclusion say 'If any of you know cause or just impediment why these persons respectively should not be joined together in Holy Matrimony, ye are to declare it.' The responsibility of the reader does not extend beyond the accurate reading of the banns and the signing of the register; any further question is a matter for the incumbent or priest-in-charge.

After the banns of marriage, if any, it is usual to read the notices. When a reader is ministering away from his home parish, these notices should be written out for him. Once again, the precaution of having read them over prior to the service is wise; you may well find you are asking people to go to a coffee morning at the home of someone whose name you cannot read, or on a day which has been omitted. If a reader is in his home parish and has any responsibility for the notices himself, let them be written down; they are likely to be both shorter and clearer.

Announce the next hymn, and move to the pulpit in a dignified manner in time to arrange your notes and switch on a pulpit light and be all composed by the time the hymn ends. The people will remain standing. Give an ascription, e.g. 'In the name of God, Father, Son and Holy Spirit. Amen'; or quote (in fact, misquote slightly) Psalm 19, verses 14 and 15 'Let the words of my mouth and the meditation of our hearts be always acceptable in thy sight, O Lord, our strength and our redeemer.' If you want to use a brief prayer before the sermon, do not say 'Let us pray' if you want the congregation to remain standing. The matter and manner of preaching is discussed elsewhere. When the sermon is over, it is normal again to use some such words as 'And now to God the Father, God the Son, and God the Holy Spirit be ascribed, as is most justly due, all might, majesty, dominion and praise from henceforth and for everymore. Amen.' Give out the number of the last hymn, wait till the singing has begun and then move to the sanctuary. Probably the collection will be brought up during this hymn; unless you know that it is the practice of the church you visit to present the collection with an audible prayer, it is best to present it silently. Turn round and say 'Let us pray'.

The reader should then kneel and say the Grace, or if the Grace has been said earlier, the prayer 'The Lord bless us and keep us ... etc.' If he wishes he may invite the congregation to join in the Grace with him. He remains kneeling for his own private prayer in which he asks God to accept his offering of leadership in worship and to forgive all that has been unworthy. He rises to his feet and follows the choir to their vestry (having checked in advance what to do with the alms-dish). There he says a prayer, dismissing the choir; he thanks the choir and bids them good-day or good-night, since in many churches choristers leave the building by a different door from the congregation. Worshippers do appreciate it if the reader goes to the church door to say good-bye as they leave. There will be many expressions of thanks for having come, the occasional comment on the sermon, but also quite likely some personal information given which should be passed on to the incumbent or priest-in-charge. This may come in the form of thanks for having prayed for the sick because an uncle has just gone into hospital for an operation. Let the reader write these bits of information down before attending to anything else, or they will be forgotten.

He returns to the vestry, takes off his robes, signs the Service Book and has a friendly word with the churchwardens. They should be ready to give him his travelling expenses, for which he should give them a receipt; that is, of course, unless the diocesan custom is that they all go through a central account. If no offer is at once made, he may ask whether they would prefer him to send an account of his travelling expenses through the Secretary of the Readers' Asociation. Readers do not receive fees for their services, but it is only right that their travelling costs should be refunded. It is not quite fair to readers in general if those more fortunately placed do not ask for their expenses.

All these small points appear at first sight rather trivial, but experience tells that it takes only one or two small things to go wrong to spoil a service. If care is taken to see that everything goes smoothly, then the meaning and structure of the service can more readily be grasped.

THE STRUCTURE OF MATINS OR MORNING PRAYER, AND EVENSONG

1. Preparation for worship. This consists of Opening Sentences, Exhortation, Confession and Absolution.
2. The Invitation to worship—Psalm 95—at Morning Prayer only.
3. Joining in worship with the pre-Christian Church in the words of the psalms.
4. The record of God's activity among men to prepare for Christ's coming.
5. The response of man. In the morning by an act of praise acknowledging the Lordship of Christ and looking forward to his coming again. In the evening, Magnificat is the response of Mary to the promise of his coming and of her special role.
6. The record of Jesus Christ and the beginnings of the Christian Church.
7. Man's response to Christ's coming. In the morning, Benedictus '... for he hath visited and redeemed his people'. In the evening, the Song of Simeon when he had seen the Christ.
8. Our own affirmation of faith in the light of the Gospel.
9. Our prayers and petitions, made in confidence because of what God has done. They open with the Family Prayer of the New Society.

To this general structure there is normally added the explanation of the Word of God in the sermon, and some more particular prayers and intercessions. It will be seen how the declaring of God's word and our response alternate; there can be seen also the linking of our prayer and our worship with what has happened in the past, in particular the singing of the psalms. The structure described above applies both to Matins and Evensong. The only material differences are in the Canticles; in the morning these are more vigorous in their praise, in the evening they are more meditative. Since the Canticles were drawn from the former morning services (Matins, Lauds and Prime) in the case of the present Matins, and from the former evening services (Vespers and Compline) in the case of Evensong, this is to be expected.

It may be valuable to the Reader to examine the parts of the services a little more closely, so that their meaning can be brought out in clearer detail.

These comments refer to the 1662 Service. The various alternative services, Series II and Series III differ in detail, but the basic structure is similar. If it is possible, it sounds better to be consistent in addressing God as either 'You' or 'Thou'.

1. *The Preparation for Worship*

This section was not to be found in the 1549 Prayer Book, presumably because confession and absolution were seen to belong to the Holy Communion and had been placed there in the 1549 Order. The present form was added in the 1552 Prayer Book, printed only before Morning Prayer but ordered to be used both then and at Evening Prayer. The call to repentance is a call to adopt a right attitude towards God at all times; if we are deliberately coming to worship, this is essential. The Exhortation goes on to put in simple language just what in our worship we are trying to do, namely:

(*a*) to thank God
(*b*) to praise God
(*c*) to hear his Word
(*d*) to make intercession.

The call to repentance leads to the General Confession, which is believed to be based on Romans 7; there are certainly many parallels in thought and language. It is interesting to realise that it was Puritan pressure which insisted that this Confession should be said kneeling, the outward attitude of the body expressing what should be the inward attitude of the mind and soul.

The Absolution or Remission of sins is to be pronounced by the priest alone. The custom of saying the Collect for the 21st Sunday after Trinity is of recent origin; in days before there were readers, for instance, a deacon conducting Matins or Evensong would at this point make a pause and then continue with the Lord's Prayer.

The Lord's Prayer is said together. This is Common, or corporate, Prayer; it is God's acceptance of us in Christ and our forgiveness through Christ, which gives us that fellowship with the Father of which the First Epistle of John speaks (I John 1.7). It is, presumably, from the same sense of corporateness that the opening Versicle misquotes Psalm 51, turning the singular into the plural; prior to the 1552 book, this was printed 'my lips' and not 'our lips'.

2. *Invitation to Worship*

Psalm 95 has a long history as such an invitation. It is used only at Morning Prayer, since the services were designed with the presumption that Christian people would be present both morning and evening. The aptness of this psalm as an opening to the worship of the day is so obvious as scarcely to need comment.

3. *The Psalms*

These were the expression of worship by those to whom the revelation of Christ had not been made. At their loftiest, they enable us to share the highest acts of praise and the deepest notes of penitence reached by those who did not know of Christ. Some psalms, on the other hand, express a zeal for justice rather than the mercy and love of God revealed in Christ; these stand as reminders of the limitations of man's judgement; they express what man without Christ felt (and often today feels) to be right and just. When we sing the psalms we are doing two things. On the one hand, we are linking ourselves with those who lived before the time of Christ and in a sense with those who live now but have never heard of him; on the other hand, we call to mind the fact that there was a time in our own lives before Christ became real to us.

The custom of singing 'Glory be to the Father, and to the Son, and to the Holy Ghost; as it was in the beginning, is now and ever shall be, world without end' at the close of each psalm, is very ancient indeed. The significance is that the God to whom pre-Christian worship was offered is not different from God in Trinity. There is, always has been and always will be one God, Father, Son and Holy Ghost.

4. The Old Testament Reading

Just as, in the psalms, our thoughts are taken back into pre-Christian times, so in the first Lesson we read of God's preparation of the world for the coming of Christ. We read of men's hopes and needs, of early interpretations of history, of the vision of God as the Giver of Law. We read of troubles being seen as the judgement of God on a nation which disobeyed him. We read of attempts to wrestle with the problem of evil. Our thanksgiving for 'the redemption of the world by our Lord Jesus Christ' and for our own inclusion in that redemption is made deeper by the Old Testament reading, for it reminds us of the world which needed and looked for redemption and of our own share in that need and hope.

5. First Canticle

Here we have mankind's response to God's promise of redemption and his fulfilment of that promise. In the canticle for Morning Prayer, the response is praise; Te Deum laudamus, 'We praise Thee, O God'. The God whom we praise is honoured by all his saints, prophets, apostles, martyrs, indeed by all his chosen people.

This same God is revealed in Christ, and so the canticle turns its praise to him. The alternative morning canticle, Benedicite omnia opera, 'O all ye works of the Lord, bless ye the Lord' is a call to the whole of creation to join in God's praise. In this canticle the name of Christ does not, of course, appear. For that reason it is well placed at this point, and appropriately is sung in Advent and Lent which are times of preparation for and looking forward to the great Festivals of the life, death and resurrection of Christ.

In the evening, the canticle Magnificat is equally appropriate. The general message of the prophets to the people of the coming Saviour gives way to the particular message to Mary that she should be the Mother of our Lord. We join, as it were with her, in her response as we praise God that Christ has been born in our hearts.

6. *The New Testament Reading*

We now move on in time to the coming of the Lord, the story of his life and work and teaching, and the building up of the Church as a consequence of his resurrection and the pouring out of his Spirit. Once again this is more than a historical record of God's saving actions. These actions are matched in men's lives and our own lives today. The drama of man's redemption in general is the same as the drama of our personal redemption. The New Testament record helps us to understand God's activity in our lives. The converse is also true, that God's activity in our own lives helps us to understand the record in the New Testament.

7. *The Second Canticle*

Now we respond to this further activity of God in Christ. At Matins we join in Benedictus, 'Blessed be the Lord God of Israel, for he *hath* visited and redeemed his people'; at Evensong the theme is the Song of Simeon when he saw the Christ with his own eyes: 'Lord now lettest thou thy servant depart in peace, according to they word. For mine eyes have seen thy salvation . . .'. Once again this can reflect our personal response to such vision of the Christ as we have ourselves experienced.

8. *The Apostles' Creed*

It is at this point in the service, when the record of God's saving activity has been read and when we have responded to God first by praise in general and finally in Christian confidence, that we join in declaring the faith of the Church to be our faith. This is the faith into which we were baptised, which we have made our own and affirm week by week. It is in the confidence of this faith that we move on to make our prayers and requests to God. This faith is part of what we have in common with fellow-Christians; it is one of our links with and in the Body of Christ. So when we have said (or sung) the Creed, we immediately open our prayers with the Lord's Prayer; this also is part of our heritage in Christ, the family prayer of the New Society.

9. *The Suffrages*

There is a pattern in these, in that they begin with prayer for the work of Christ and end with prayer for the influence of the Holy Spirit in the lives of individuals. The sequence is simple:

1. The work of man's salvation
2. The sovereign (In America, 'O Lord, save the State')
3. The clergy
4. The people of God
5. The peace of the world
6. The Holy Spirit in our lives

The structure of the concluding prayers after the third Collect is similar and provides a pattern which can be followed if, as is customary, other occasional prayers are used instead.

10. The Collects

The Collect for the Day provides a special theme for prayer. The total sequence of these Collects provides a wide range of thoughts and concern which acts to correct any lack of emphasis, or neglect on one side or another, which might occur if the choice of prayers were left wholly to one minister in a congregation. The fixed (second and third) Collects, both morning and evening, need no comment; those in the morning ask for grace and protection to live and work according to God's will, while those in the evening ask for similar grace and protection to finish our course and then sleep in peace.

If this structure of Morning Prayer and of Evensong is clearly grasped, it can be explained by the reader in his teaching and brought out by the way he conducts the service.

6
Preaching

PREACHING is a ministry of the Word. To minister is to be a servant, and so the preacher is a servant of the Word. He may be master of many things and, in preaching, he does well to try to be master of his information; but when he comes to preach a sermon it is as servant and not as master. He is a servant twice over. He is a servant of the Word, that is to say a servant of Christ; for the 'Word was made flesh and dwelt among us'. He is also a servant of those to whom he preaches. He is a servant when reading the Bible, either in his home or in a church. There is a sense in which by criticism and study, he may be judged a master of some books. But in the Scriptures, however rightly he exercises his critical faculty, he only understands if he is willing to be subject and not master.

Preaching is presenting Christ, the Word of God, in such a way that men will encounter him. They may reject him as a result of the encounter. It is the preacher's aim that men will not reject Christ because of any distorted way in which he was presented. The preacher will constantly pray 'Let not those that seek thee be confounded through me' (Psalm 69.6). He will try to present Christ to the mind and to the heart, to the imagination and to the will. When addressing the mind, however, he is not writing an essay or delivering a theological lecture. When addressing the will, he is not giving an instruction in morals but making clearer the effect of Christ on the moral judgements of men. In Christ there is the gift of life and also a challenge to offer life. News is accompanied by challenge; demand is accompanied by the offer of the means to respond. The proclaiming of Christ by the preacher will include both these notes if it is to be true to him.

The character of preaching and the content of the message will vary according to the occasion when the sermon is to be delivered. There are preachers who address the same congregation Sunday after Sunday. They can well afford to limit the range of any particular sermon since they know that they will almost certainly have the chance to speak on a different aspect of the same theme another week. Each sermon can be seen as part of a balanced spiritual diet for a regular congregation. Whether a sequence of sermons is announced as a course or not, there can be a connected sequence of themes; the many facets of the Person of Christ and the many steps in the Christian life can be spoken of in turn. On some occasions of the year, however, there will be visitors in the congregation who come to worship infrequently and for them a different approach is needed. The occasions when such visitors largely come are the principal Festivals of the Christian Year together with such times as Harvest Thanksgiving or Remembrance Sunday. On such occasions the preacher's theme is provided for him. On the other occasions he may ensure a balance in the sequence of sermons through using the Gospel or Epistle or Collect for the day, or the lessons appointed for Matins and Evensong, as the basis of his sermon.

The reader is at a slight disadvantage in this regard since about one-third of his preaching is likely to be in a church other than that of his home parish, and not as part of a regular sequence. He is not going to see that particular congregation again Sunday after Sunday. Since he is unable to redress any imbalance in his sermon by what he says the following Sunday, there must be great care to see that his sermon is complete in itself. This does not mean that he will try to discuss the whole of the Christian faith and its relevance in every department of life. His subject-matter may well be chosen because of its connection with the particular Sunday in the Christian Year, but the manner of its treatment will be affected by the fact that the preacher cannot, as it were, go on next week.

Once the reader has grasped the nature of the occasion and of the place where he is to preach, he must choose the subject matter of his sermon. He will realise that by the time he reaches the pulpit his subject will be very familiar to him but as yet unknown to the congregation. For this reason it will help the congregation if the hymns are chosen with the subject in mind, and still more if the subject matter arises out of the Lessons or Collect for the day. Brief introductions to the Lessons can also prepare the minds of the people for the sermon that is to follow. Once the theme for the address is chosen, it should be studied thoroughly. If the theme arises out of the Lessons, how does it fit into the whole pattern of the drama of man's redemption? In other words the passage chosen, if a text is used, must be studied in its context and the similarities and differences between that context and the local and world situation today considered. What did the passage mean to the people to whom it was originally addressed, and is that meaning relevant to us now? This will involve the use of commentaries and books for background reading.

The reader is commissioned to preach about God. He is not charged to teach Syrian geography or to talk at length about local farming in the first century. There are times when a knowledge of these things is useful for an understanding of a parable or a prophecy. If the preacher has been speaking about the Good Shepherd, or the Parable of the Lost Sheep, the congregation should go away knowing more of the love and care of God for his people without having been distracted by a lengthy discussion on how sheep were kept in folds in the Holy Land at the time of Christ. Again, the reader is not commissioned to expound his own opinions on public or private morals; he is commissioned to proclaim the Gospel and to expound the Scriptures. When the Scriptures place public and private morals under judgement, he is right to say so with all the clarity and all the charity at his command.

The preacher has the privilege of being the servant of the Word and of declaring the good news of Christ to the people for whom he lived and died. It is up-to-date news. The Bible may tell of Christ's birth and life and death and ressurection and ascension; it also tells the beginning of the story of the community which was empowered by the Holy Spirit to continue Christ's work. The life and witness of that community, the Church, is part of the good news. The preacher has a message which is a matter of life and death; indeed more than that, for he can speak of eternal life and point the way to men to find it. Let his message be clear, let it be relevant in its presentation but, above all, let it be big enough.

What the preacher says and what the listener remembers may be quite different things. The preacher has news to tell which is important and universally relevant; his task is to present it in such a way that its importance and relevance will be grasped. The reader has a message from God and about God. He has the news that Christ is alive, that Christ reigns and that he is present. He speaks with authority, not because of his own attainments and abilities but because of God's revelation. His message on Easter Day is not that taking everything into account it seems reasonable to think that something unusual must have happened. On the contrary he is charged to say with confidence 'Jesus lives!' and to explain some of the conclusions to which the hymn with that opening comes.

The reader will preach out of his own experience and conviction. He will preach that Christ has overcome the world, and that death and sin have been conquered, because of his experience of the power of Christ in his life. He will preach that the character of God is unchangeable, his will unchanging, and his love unchanging because he knows this for himself. In a world of so much mobility, unrest and change, this is good news. He will preach that the Holy Spirit can be relied upon for inspiration and for power and he will speak out of his own conviction of the means by which man experiences that inspiration and power. He will speak of the power of prayer and will teach how power can come alive. At the Friends Meeting House in Cambridge at a time when experiments in the Cavendish Laboratory were pointing to the possibilities of nuclear fission, Professor Eddington rose to speak. It was true, he said, that the physical power which scientists had shown they could release was beyond most people's imagination. He was equally convinced, he continued, that the power of the Spirit of God which could be ours by prayer was stronger than any power that man could release. Such comments carry conviction only when it is evident that the speaker knows what he is talking about. The preacher does not need to catalogue the occasions when his prayers have been answered in order to convey his belief in the value of prayer.

To be of value, a sermon must be in the language of the hearer. In simple terms this is obvious. If the hearers do not understand English, then clearly an interpreter is needed. The interpreter will translate what is said into a language which the hearers will understand. Precise translation of words may not be possible or, if possible, may not convey the meaning intended. In the language of some African tribes, there are no words to convey the idea 'near' or 'far'. Thus, if the preacher explains that the prodigal son had gone 'far away', the interpreter will at some length explain that he had walked into the country and that if he had called for his mother she could not hear. This they will understand. This is not only possible in their language, but intelligible to their minds. A sermon must be not only in the language, but in the thought-form of the hearer. Another example may be taken from Africa, where I was about to preach to some Matabele about forgiveness using the passage about a hundred pence and ten thousand talents. A preliminary word with the interpreter revealed that pence, talents and large numbers were unintelligible. A sermon about a man who was forgiven a debt of ten cows, but insisted on the repayment of three hens, was understood.

The reader will therefore have studied his message and the Scripture on which it is based in a way which will bring it to life in the minds of his hearers. Commentaries, Bibles with cross-references, and modern translations will all help to bring out the meaning. When he has grasped the meaning as best he can, he will look for ways to illustrate that meaning in terms of the experience of his hearers. It is natural that the Parables of Jesus should be in terms of the everyday life of first-century Palestine. The illustrations used by the preacher in an industrial parish or a big city will be in terms of the everyday surroundings of his hearers. Consider the story of the hospital staff nurse called Jennifer and an orderly in the ward called Muriel. Jennifer took up nursing because she was concerned about sick people; Muriel was only concerned to earn some money before she got married. One day there was a fire in the hospital and Jennifer rushed into the ward to carry out the patients. She called to Muriel to help, but Muriel replied 'It's useless, Jenny, you will get killed if you go into that inferno', and she ran to safety. Jennifer therefore went in on her own and brought out the patients. When the fire brigade had come and put out the flames, they found Jennifer's body scorched and lifeless. At the funeral, the chaplain opened his Bible at St John Chapter 10, 'Jesus said, I am the good staff nurse; the good staff nurse gives her life for the patients'. The reader may well not want to use such a story in just those terms, though they are terms which would be easily understood; there are more staff nurses in Liverpool or London than there are shepherds. Whatever illustrations are used, let them be in terms understood by both preacher and congregation. The reader has in this regard some advantage over many of the clergy, for his daily life involves him in the tensions of the secular world in a way which the clergy do not share. He does well to use that involvement to enrich his preaching, using but not going beyond his experience. In this way the preaching of the reader and of the clergyman balance and supplement one another, each being only a part of the total spoken witness of the Church.

It was said by Canon B. K. Cunningham that a good sermon was about God and about twenty minutes. The present tendency is for the sermon to be about ten or fifteen minutes, but it can still be about God. There should be a definite subject and a clear aim. At the end of the sermon it should be possible for each member of the congretion to give some positive answer to the question 'What have I learned about the ways of God?'. Since the congregation have to listen to the sermon and cannot go back and read the last paragraph again, the preacher may present his main theme in various forms. This would be to make the sermon like a piece of music 'Variations on a theme by . . .'. One variation may appeal more to the mind, another more to the heart or the will or the imagination. Having chosen or considered his theme, let the Reader ask himself a number of questions, e.g.:

Why do I believe this to be true?
What led me first to realise the importance of this truth?

In other words he will consider what difference this truth makes to his daily life, his aim and purpose in life, his prayers and his worship. He can then go on to ask himself whether his hearers are likely to believe this truth already, or whether they realise its importance. On the answer to this question will depend whether the sermon is more an explanation or an exploration of a truth. He will consider whether others are likely to be led to grasp this truth in the same way that he was led. He will go on to ask himself what difference a grasp of this truth would make to others; for instance, what difference would a firmly-held conviction of the Fatherhood of God make to trade union or employers' policies?

Every sermon, including an expository sermon, should have relevance *now*, for God meets us in the actual happenings of every day life. Further, divine truths come to us with both support and challenge. God does not ask us to do anything for him without providing the means for doing it; nor does he give us any grace or blessing for our private enjoyment, but expects us to use it to further his will on earth. A sermon, therefore, should reveal these two sides of divine truth. For example, a missionary sermon on the command 'Go ye therefore . . . ' should include the truth 'I am with you always'. The application of the truth should preferably be described in social and not merely individual terms. It is not part of the thought-form of today to ask 'What must I do to be saved?' but rather to ask the question in the plural. Man's interdependence has been so forcibly brought home to him in the last century that he thinks of salvation in social terms first. Personal salvation in a doomed world is not the desire of many, but the redemption of society itself is. Thus the relevance of the sin of the world to the Cross of Christ is easy to explain. Since no individual can opt out of responsibility for the sin of the world, he cannot disclaim any involvement in the Crucifixion. The reverse is true. If the Crucifixion is the victory of love in the face of man's fullest rejection, the power of love is seen as greater than the power of man's sin. If this applies at the corporate level, it will also apply at the individual level. The reader will be wise to consider the social application of most truths first, and then to pass on to the personal application, rather than the other way round.

When preparing a sermon, the reader will naturally think out what illustrations to use and how many there shall be. Clearly they must be designed to help the congregation grasp the truth which is the subject of the sermon. Therefore the illustration must not only not be far-fetched, but must be easily understood and carry the ring of truth. A danger to be avoided is to use a good story and make it the burden of the message instead of an illustration of the message. This will divert the attention of the hearer from the central message, unless the story itself enshrines the truth. Some people will go home remembering only the story, especially if it has been well told. This does not matter as long as the story really conveys the message in itself. In such a case the story acts like an illustration in a book on flowers or birds; even if the reader only looks at the pictures, he learns much to help him identify a specimen and also to have an increasing awareness of the beauty of nature. In other books, such as novels or books on chemistry and mathematics, it is not sufficient just to look at the pictures.

Illustration is different from application. The Christian Gospel makes a difference to life and the sermon should indicate what that difference is. A sermon on the use of the number twelve, the multiple of the heavenly three and the earthly four, might be very interesting but would not be particularly helpful to a person who needs strength against temptation, guidance in perplexity or encouragement to keep going. The application must be within the grasp of the hearers, and not just point a moral to people who are not there and cannot be touched by the words even indirectly. Thus a sermon on Jewish shepherds and Arab wise men worshipping the new-born Christ may well have an application to Middle East politics. Its relevance to the people of a city parish, or to the worshippers in a village church, needs to be spelled out as well if the sermon is to be of real value.

In general the only visual aid the congregation are going to have is the reader himself. His pulpit manners and mannerisms, his use of gesture and so on, can either hinder or help the congregation to attend to what he has to say. In general only other people, and very honest people they must be, can point out to the preacher the mannerisms which distract attention. Continual looking at a watch, putting on and taking off spectacles, scratching one's neck or stroking one's beard, fiddling with one's notes or perpetual use of the same gesture can be almost guaranteed to prevent the congregation listening to what is being said. Most worshippers are too polite to mention the offending mannerism, but if the reader has a wife and family they can help his ministry by being ruthlessly honest in this matter.

When the reader has prepared the main theme of his sermon, decided what illustrations to use and where they shall come, and sketched out how the truth being declared is likely to apply to the lives of the congregation, he has to decide just how the sermon shall begin and end. It was Canon Ireson who compared a sermon with a sherry party. If in the first minute or so you meet someone you know, who introduces you to someone else, the party is interesting; but if you stand around for two minutes without seeing anybody you have ever met before, for you the party is dead. In the first two minutes of a sermon there should be a familiar and easily recognisable thought. The first familar thought does not always need to be outstandingly arresting, for the congregation are willing to attend for the first two minutes in case the preacher has something to say. If in the first two minutes the preacher is talking above their heads (or beneath their intelligence) or is discussing some topic about which as yet they know nothing, the listeners will unconsciously switch off their attention and think about other things. Abstract concepts are difficult to grasp and should be avoided in the opening of a sermon. For example, a simple tale of a couple who had overcome a series of ups and downs in their married life provides a better opening to a sermon on Christian marriage than a dissertation on loyalty.

Similarly the end of the sermon should be simple and definite. When the sermon is finished it should end. Readers should copy the curate who said 'And in conclusion . . .' and concluded, rather than the vicar who said 'Lastly . . .' and lasted. A born teacher who was ordained later in life used to tell the congregation in two or three simple sentences what his sermon was about; he then preached it; he then reminded his congregation of the points he had tried to make. At least everybody knew what had been said and would remember. This is most important. The spoken word matters more than many people realise. The medical practitioner knows that whatever he may have done to help a patient, probably the first question the patient's wife will ask is 'What did the doctor say?' It is a badly constituted sermon if the hearer cannot give a proper answer to a similar question.

It has already been said that the subject-matter of the sermon may well arise out of the Lessons or the Collect for the day. It has also been said that the sermon should not go beyond the experience of the preacher. This does not mean that he may not use the ideas of others; almost every preacher does this, consciously or unconsciously. What is important is that the ideas of others should be so grasped by the reader that they become part of his own understanding of the truth. In Church newspapers and in one or two national daily papers, there are to be found articles related to the Lessons, Collect, Epistle or Gospel for the Sunday following. Some of these have since been published in book form as, for instance, the volumes *Reflections on the Collects,*[1] *Reflections on the Epistles*[2] and *Reflections on the Gospels*[3] by Bishop J. W. C. Wand, which are collections of articles he wrote for the *Church Times. The Reader* magazine also contains sermon thoughts for the month. In addition there are books of sermon outlines such as *Preaching at the Parish Communion*[4] by Prebendary D. W. Clevereley Ford and the many volumes in the series *Preaching through the Christian Year*[5]. Alternatively there are books designed for private reading or an aid to prayer which may bring a thought to the tired mind of a reader who is asked to preach at short notice, which can happen only too easily when an incumbent is taken ill suddenly. Indeed this is a problem a reader is more likely to face than the average clergyman.

Clearly these sermon outlines, or full-length sermons, cannot be used as they stand. Quite apart from the obvious topical and personal references, the language, the illustrations and the whole emphasis belong to the writer. There is, however, a simple technique which can be used. If the outline, or short sermon, is on a Lesson or Collect, then the first step is to read the Lesson or Collect carefully for ourselves. Then read the outline two or three times; if possible aloud. If the outline sermon is going to prove of any real value to us, we should by this time be able to write down on a blank sheet of paper two or three points which we believe to be true and relevant. These then provide the basis of a sermon which we construct and which is ours and not that of the original writer. The illustrations will be ours and not his; quite possibly the application will be different, coming out of our experience and not his. What we have done is to strip the original down to three points, which we have then reclothed in words of our own. The finished product should still stand up to the tests already

[1] A. R. Mowbray.
[2] ibid.
[3] ibid.
[4] ibid.
[5] ibid.

suggested; it should be about God, it should express the conviction of the preacher in the language of the hearer and it should explain the difference it makes in life and thought and prayer.

Preaching is service of the Word, and the Word was made flesh. 'We preach not ourselves, but Christ Jesus as Lord'. The ultimate aim, whatever our method or our source of ideas, is so to present the living Christ that others may love him more and serve him better. The confidence of the preacher comes not from knowing which verses in scripture to underline, but in knowing more about him of whom those verses speak. It is not enough for the preacher to know the 23rd Psalm; he must also know the Shepherd.

7
The Reader and His Books

QUITE naturally, in order to gain the certificate referred to in Chapter 3, the reader will have to study a number of the books suggested in the Study Guide on each section of the syllabus. It is clear from these Study Guides that the course of training is intended to be an introduction to a life-time of further reading and gaining the certificate does not mark the end of one's studies. A glance at the bookshelves of a reader, as of a clergyman, will indicate how much chance he is giving to his mind to grow.

One of the problems, of course, is to find the time necessary for reading and to know how much time to give. There is a simple rule which, I believe, the reader should make his own, that is, to give as much time to taking in as he spends in giving out. The reader is offering some of his time in the service of the Church, and to conduct Evensong in a church other than in his own parish may easily mean the use of two or three hours on a Sunday evening. If the rule about reading suggested were adopted, the reader would match that time with two or three hours of reading on another evening during the week. The freshness of the mind which would result would affect the quality of preaching and the conduct of services for the better. There may be times when the reader would have to decline invitations to preach if acceptance would result in more time being spent giving out than taking in. His standing and commission as a reader in the Church requires that he should keep up to date as far as he can, broadening his mind and enlarging his knowledge. To those who think and say they do not have the time, the suggestion may be made to put 'Reading' in one's dairy as an engagement and therefore to decline any other engagement suggested for that evening because one is busy.

Reading is a way of meeting other people at second-hand; the other people are the authors of the books. When we meet other people, we listen as well as speak; we learn what they have to say about this or that. If we are interested in a subject we shall want to know what a variety of people have to say about it. If we are interested in a person we shall want to know what he has to say about a variety of subjects. When, therefore, the entry 'Reading' appears in my diary it means that I have an interview (at second-hand) with one or more people about whose opinions and experiences I wish to know more. The fact that these people share a concern for what matters most in life makes this indirect meeting all the more exhilarating.

There are so many books which have been written about Jesus Christ and the Christian religion, as well as books less specifically 'religious' but of general interest, that the reader may well ask where to start and how to establish some sort of balance in his reading. Clearly he needs to know the scriptures and as much about them as possible, not for the purpose of passing examinations or because he is required to preach, but because they enshrine the record of particular dealings of God with men. They convey the record of God's redeeming acts which provide the ground of the Christian's faith. The reader will therefore not neglect to read the Scriptures themselves, and use commentaries and other books which will help him to understand the Scriptures better. He will be wise to turn to different translations so that the familiar forms of words will not hide from him some slant of meaning which he may not have noticed. There are many translations which have been published in recent years. Among them the reader will find himself turning with profit to the Revised Standard Version, the New English Bible, the Jerusalem Bible and the Good News Bible (Today's English Version). In addition to translation of the Bible, the reader should have available a good commentary. Commentaries are expensive but the reader who is able to afford to purchase *Peake's Revised Com-*

mentary (1962)[1] will then have at hand a book which will help him for many years. There are a number of books which are not strictly commentaries but which open up the meaning of the books of the Bible. A book such as William Temple's *Readings in St John's Gospel*[2] is a classic of this kind.

Secondly, the reader will want to know more and more about how God has acted in history. His limited study of Church History for the General Readers' Certificate will, it is hoped, have made him want to see more clearly where God has guided the Church and also when and where the Church has not been responsive to his guidance. He will not, of course, fall into the temptation of thinking that Church History is the record of God's activity and secular history the record of man's activity. He will realise that God is active in the affairs of man as a whole. Historical books, including historical novels, will form part of his general reading. In specifically Church affairs, he will want to read of trends in the Church today and its relation with the world. He would do well to know what the Second Vatican Council was all about by reading the volume of essays of the Anglican observers, edited by Canon B. C. Pawley[3]. He would do well to read what Harvey Cox has to say about *The Secular City*[4] or Bishop David Sheppard in *Built as a City*.[5] Quite apart from books of this kind, and those standard works which he will have studied for his examination, the reader will want to have a Church newspaper to keep him familiar with what is happening in the Church of England today. He will also profit by reading up-to-date reports from the Missionary Societies, so that what is happening in the Church overseas may be familiar to him, and the journal Theology.

Thirdly there are books, on all sorts of subjects, which open our eyes to see old truths in a new way and to grasp new ideas. To read these is like meeting new people whose ideas are refreshing.

[1] Thos. Nelson [2] MacMillan (St. Martins Library Edition, 1961).
[3] *The Second Vatican Council*, O.U.P. [4] S.C.M. (1966)
[5] Hodder & Stoughton (1974)

One of the reasons why Holiday Conferences are so popular is that we get away from familiar surroundings to see new places and meet new people and hear new ideas. We may not always agree with these people and their ideas, but we go home refreshed for having met them. In the same way there are books which might well be described as eye-openers. The reader may not always agree with everything the author writes, but this is quite beside the point. It is important to read books by authors of a different outlook from our own, otherwise we ourselves grow into one-sided people. To gain a balanced view about matters of doctrine or Church History or the understanding of the Bible, it is good to learn what those of different denominational allegiance have to say. But the great value in the kind of book to which I refer is that it puts the familiar truth in fresh language. At the time of its publication *Honest to God*[1] by Bishop Robinson made many people think afresh about familiar truths; in a less popular manner Professor Lampe's *God as Spirit*[2] has done the same more recently. In a different way, H. A. William's *The True Wilderness*[3] contains little that is controversial, but speaks of experiences of God which for some have been either unseen or unrecognised. In yet another way books such as Archbishop Ramsey's *God, Christ and the World*[4] and Hans Küng's *On Being a Christian*[5] open our eyes to the richness of familiar truths. These refresh the mind and so, one hopes, make the reader a more interesting person when in his turn he speaks to others.

Fourthly there are those books written not just by interesting people but about interesting people. Biographies are written with this very intent, that we shall meet the subject of the book at second-hand. Some of these biographies the reader may well want to have on his own shelves so that he can turn to them again and again. He will also want to use the Public Library to enlarge the circle of second-hand acquaintances beyond that number determined by the limits of his purse. Through bio-

[1] S.C.M. (1963). [2] O.U.P. (1977) [3] Constable (1965).
[4] S.C.M. (1969). [5] Collins

graphies and autobiographies he can come to know, as it were, Church leaders such as William Temple, Archbishop Garbett and Bishop Hensley Henson; he can learn of great explorers such as Captain Scott and Dr Wilson of the Antarctic, or great Christians overseas such as Apolo or Gladys Aylward. The list would be unending.

Finally, the reader will profit by sharing the thoughts of those who can give him new insights into the life of prayer. By this I do not mean books of prayers only, though the reader will gradually build up a small collection of these both for private and public use. Prayer is at the very heart of the life of a Christian, and the reader will want to do all he can to learn from others how they have enriched their own prayers so that he may share their richness for himself. The reader is in a position to help others in this vital matter and needs to be as well equipped as possible. Books about prayer which the reader would find helpful might include Sister Edna Mary's *This World and Prayer*,[1] Neville Ward's *The Use of Praying*,[2] Archbishop Coggan's *Prayers of the New Testament*[3] and Fr. Mark Gibbard's *Dynamics of Prayer*.[4] Again, readers (and clergy) would derive much benefit from Balthazar's *Prayer*.[5] Then there are books of prayers designed not for public use but to give new vision to the individual how to pray, such as Michel Quoist's *Prayers of Life*[6] or Dick William's *God-thoughts*.[7] The list could be extended almost endlessly, and the reader's bookshelf will reveal how he is equipping himself to grow in experience in this important area of his Christian life.

The suggestions just made are but an introduction to the whole subject of the reader and his reading of books. The important thing is that he should continually be keeping his mind alert by taking in the ideas of other people. To decide what to read is one thing; to vary the method of reading according to what is read is another. There are some books which can be picked up, read for

[1] S.P.C.K. (1965) [2] Epworth Press (1967) [3] H. & S.
[4] Mowbray [5] Chapman (1963) [6] Gill & MacMillan
[7] Falcon Books (1969)

a short time and then put down again for a while. Others need to be read in more prolonged stretches. The pace of reading will also vary greatly according to the type of book. Perhaps both the pace of reading and the amount read at a time vary with the person reading, so that what seems natural and easy to one person will be tiresome to another. Some people can read best when alone and in silence; others of my close acquaintance deliberately turn on the radio to a musical programme, or play records of a symphony, to prevent themelves being distracted by other sounds.

When reading the Bible and commentaries, the reader will want to be as undisturbed as possible. Some of this study may be in preparation for preaching or leading a study-circle. For this he will use pen and paper to make notes. But his reading of the Bible will not begin and end there. If he believes that God speaks to others through the Scriptures, and that as a reader he is called to help others hear God's Word, then he must put himself in the place of a listener. At his Confirmation, prayer was made that he might grow in knowledge and obedience of God's Word. Knowledge and obedience go together in this regard, and for an understanding of the scripture he who reads places himself under the judgement of the Word. The length of time given to this kind of reading of the Bible matters less than the unhurried and undistracted concentration. From time to time, the reader will find parts of the Bible take on a freshness of meaning when a whole Epistle is read at one sitting. This is especially so when a modern translation is used. On the other hand, when a detailed commentary is used, the reader may well find that after quite a short time his mind is getting tired and he is wise not to go on but to recapitulate the points that have been made and then to turn to quite another kind of reading.

History and historical novels lend themselves to faster reading and to being read for longer periods at a time. The aim here is to obtain an overall picture and to see the relation between many events. Biographies, on the other hand, vary so much that no one rule could apply. In some cases long periods of fast reading are needed to grasp the life as a whole. In other cases and more often, one reads a biography as one develops a friendship in frequent short periods of meeting. In a friendship between two people, they derive pleasure in recalling incidents of the past; so in reading biographies, one can derive pleasure by turning again to familiar episodes and refreshing the memory of significant incidents. The books which I have described as eye-openers can also be read profitably in short spells. In some of them new ideas come tumbling after one another and it is good to give each time to be grasped before passing on to the next.

Books on prayer call for quietness and concentration, and usually are best read slowly. The reader may well find himself wanting to pause for reflection, and then may want to go back and read the last part again. Time and conditions should allow reading to turn into prayer itself.

Few readers will be able to buy all the books they would like to read, and generous use should be made of the Public Library service, which is always most ready to obtain books which are requested. Where possible, a deanery or archdeaconry Book Club for readers is invaluable. This can be organised on the basis of an annual subscription, and the books circulated from one member to the next. If a grant can be made from Diocesan Readers' Association funds, so much the better; and use can be made of the Bray Library if the group complies with the conditions. A dozen readers linked together in a deanery can, by using these facilities and at modest cost to themselves, have access to enough books each year to keep their minds alert and their interests wide. If readers were less hesitant to claim their travelling expenses when visiting parishes other than their own, and were to use part of that money on books for themselves and for a deanery library, they and others would be better equipped.

8

The Reader at Prayer

A READER, like a clergyman, is necessarily involved in spending much time conducting public worship and in preparing for services. The things that go on inside church buildings are his particular concern. However true it may be that minister and people offer an act of worship together, there is a great difference between the approach of the minister and that of the worshipper in the congregation. The worshipper may make the prayers and praises his own, but he had no part in choosing them nor in the manner in which they were presented as a vehicle of worship. The reader or clergyman knowing that he is responsible for the conduct of a service the following Sunday will spend time and thought preparing for it. He must ask himself what prayers will have meaning in the context of that act of worship, and prepare them accordingly. Books of prayers suitable for public use, with a limited variety of form and usually of a general character, are part of his stock in trade. His mind becomes more and more geared to the needs of public corporate worship, and the forms of prayer suitable to that form of worship tend to occupy a larger place in his own devotional life. A similar tendency is liable to show itself in his use of the Bible. As he reads his Bible, there is likely to be at the back of his mind the thought that this or that passage has a message which can be used to help others at a service in church. In other words there is a temptation to regard the Bible as a book to be used for our own purposes, even though that purpose is to help others come to faith and find their fulfilment within the fellowship of the church. There is nothing wrong in this, but it needs to be balanced by a reading of the Bible in which there is a deliberate placing of ourselves under the judgement of the Word, and it is not impossible for the two things to happen at the same time.

As the reader finds himself preparing to lead public worship he naturally finds himself thinking and reading and praying with the Church in the sequence of the Christian year. There is a sense in which every Christian prays with the Church, but the clergyman and the reader do this with growing awareness. This is particularly true if he uses the Daily Office, or even such parts of it as the psalms for the day and either one or all of the lessons appointed. One of the strong features of societies such as the Scripture Union, the Bible Reading Fellowship, and the International Bible Reading Association is that hundreds of thousands of other people are reading the same passage and this provides a common bond. The same applies in the use of the Anglican Cycle of Prayer or the Prayer Calendar of ones own diocese. There is great strength in this corporate sense, but there is needed the balance which comes from strong, personal and individual prayer. There is a wrong form of detachment from the Christian Body, an individualism which makes light of our membership one of another. The realisation of our essential fellowship in the Body of Christ has corrected what used to be a false emphasis on 'making my Communion' by a greater emphasis on the fact that it is the Communion of the Church in which we share. There is also, however, a right form of detachment in which we realise our aloneness before God, our personal involvement in the sin of the world, our personal indebtedness to Christ for our salvation; in which we can pour out our own hopes and fears, make our own particular intercessions and express our own especial gratitude for individual blessings. The most important relationship the reader has is his relationship with God, and this finds expression in his private prayers. The danger of corporate prayer crowding out private prayer is a danger with which every clergyman lives. The danger may not be as great for the reader, but being less obvious it may be more subtle and less easily recognised.

Of what elements should this private prayer consist, through which our relationship with God is maintained and strengthened? There are many books about prayer, but just what can we do to make our prayers more full of meaning? Clearly there is no pattern of private prayer that will suit every person. The thoughts which follow are suggested in the hope that they may be found by some readers, at least, to provide a framework on which their daily private prayer can be built. They may prove helpful to readers in teaching others about prayer.

1. Prayer is directing our whole person towards God; it is an activity of the whole self, body, mind and spirit. It takes place, as far as we are concerned, on earth and in time. Jesus taught 'when you pray, go into your room and shut the door and pray to your Father who is in secret' (Matt. 6.6). A time and a place need choosing for prayer to be without distraction. There cannot be a rule common to all; there can be a rule for each person. Within the selected time and place, body, mind and spirit are to be directed towards God. It is so easy to forget the body and to think that the body can be doing one thing, so long as the mind is thinking godly thoughts. But if we try to pray while part of ourselves, namely our body, is doing something else, not all our attention is being directed to God. This does not mean that we cannot pray as we walk, or drive, or listen to music or as we write a letter. What is suggested is that there must be some regular occasions when we try to direct every part of ourselves and our attention to God. The position of the body is then part of our prayer, whether sitting or kneeling. If we say our prayers only after getting into bed after a tiring day, the devil knows he has won already.

2. The use of outward signs and aids to attention are all part of the body being brought into the activity of prayer. Some people use the sign of the cross; this is a physical reminder of what they are doing and of the God to whom they intend to pray. It is an aid to attention. Others will use some visual aid such as a crucifix, or a picture or some other outward reminder which

helps to direct attention. It does not matter much what way is used, but let there be a way. Again since the objective is to direct our whole attention to God, let the outward symbol or picture or words be as much related to God in himself and as little as possible to ourselves and our needs. For instance, the first verse of 'Holy, holy, holy, Lord God Almighty' is all about God and not ourselves; alternatively 'My God, how wonderful thou art, Thy majesty how bright' contains very little of self. Let each person select his own words, choosing those which come most readily to mind and are most easily remembered. The use of a selected posture, an outward sign or symbol or visual aid, and of words which speak of God, help to direct the mind to reach out to him and take from the mind some of its own anxieties.

3. God is so great and beyond our grasp that no one thought about him is sufficient to give us even a remote picture of him. Our prayers will quickly be distorted if there is a perpetual sameness in our thoughts about God, and the monotony of such prayers is likely to kill any efforts we make to grow in the life of prayer. God discloses himself to us in so many different ways, that we should make use of this vast variety and let our approach to him one day be of one form and another day be of quite another form. Christians who think of God only as the Forgiver of sins, or only as Creator of the world, or only in some other particular way, quickly become one-sided creatures. This is where the reader will find the sequence of themes and readings associated with the Christian Year so helpful. During each week some different revelation of God becomes the object of our attention; day by day we think of some different facet of the character and activity of God. In this way each day we see God a little more in his greatness, and there is a variety in our prayers which fights against dullness and staleness. This is not to identify the Daily Office with our private prayer, but rather to suggest that part of the great value of saying the Daily Office can overflow into our time of private prayer.

4. If the first step in our prayers is to think about God as much

as possible and about ourselves as little as possible, it becomes easier to distinguish praise and adoration from thanksgiving. To take a very elementary example, suppose we give to a child a present, the response might well be 'Oh, how lovely! Thank you very much.' In respect of God's gifts, the first thought leads to adoration and the second is thanksgiving. To see cherry trees in full bloom in a city suburb, or a sunset in the Fens, to see a smile on the face of one of God's children in a city slum or to wonder at the beauty of the crocuses on the Cambridge Backs, is to be on the road to adoration. Here again variety in the thought that leads to adoration enlarges our thinking and enlivens our prayers. This kind of variety is to be found in the Canticle *Benedicite*, 'O all ye works of the Lord, bless ye the Lord'. Adoration is expressed when the mind and soul lead on from some thought about God's self-disclosure to say 'My God, how wonderful thou art'.

5. Thanksgiving brings self into the picture, 'Now thank we all our God'. We thank him because we are the richer, or the stronger or the better, because of what he has done or given. Thanksgiving is looking at something either that we have or that has happened and being glad about it for God's sake. If we look at thanksgiving this way, then we shall find penitence and thanksgiving go very closely together. As we look round on the world, there are some things about which we are glad and others about which we must be very sorry. The child on whose face we saw a smile, which gave us joy and led us to give God praise and thanks for the joy it gave us, may live in a slum dwelling unfit for human habitation about which we have no joy or pleasure. About this last fact we are distressed, even if there seems little we can do about it at the time. Penitence is looking at something we have done or that has happened and being sorry about it for Christ's sake. This means that we look round on the world at large or the events of the day as we have experienced them; we sort out the things of which we think into those of which we are glad for Christ's sake and those about which we are distressed for his sake.

There may be some things about which we are sorry, our own failures or disappointments or humiliation for example, but which may become part of God's plan for our lives. It is easy to confuse annoyance with ourselves at having failed to achieve something we wanted to do with penitence. Equally, something may have happened which gives us great personal pleasure which is a hindrance to the doing of God's will; the success we seem to have achieved may be making us trust too much in our own power, and may make us seek our own ends instead of God's. So when we sort out events and experiences, we give thanks or are distressed not for our sake but because they reflect or hinder the will of God.

The factor of variety applies powerfully at this point in prayer. It was, I think, Charles Simeon who tried to thank God for something different every day without repeating himself. The exercise is not difficult and its effect is to enlarge our vision of the goodness of God. The use of a notebook helps the exercise to be taken seriously; the botanist or stamp-collector catalogues his finds with a zeal which sets an example for the man who wants to learn to pray. For instance, we sit down and listen to a record of a Beethoven Symphony; the event provides us with occasion to thank God that we can hear, that Beethoven lived at all and wrote that music in particular, for the inventors of records and record-players, for musicians and conductors and so on. There are a dozen or more things which are the occasion of thanksgiving. This exercise in listing the variety of things for which to thank is an exercise which increases our awareness of the generosity of God. Of course, the same applies the other way round to the things that are unfortunate and unhappy and sinful. We do not need to commit a new sin each day to discover the variety of sinfulness; in many situations there will be many factors which we should regret for Christ's sake. There may be some besetting sin of which we are so conscious that we become blind to the very many other things in our lives for which we ought to be penitent; if this exercise of listing the things we regret for Christ's sake makes us realise how many things hinder God's will, it will be worth while.

In thanksgiving and in penitence, it is not necessary only to be personal. We can thank God for his blessings to us and to all men (as the General Thanksgiving says) which means that we can include in our list blessings to others which we do not ourselves share. This really makes thanksgiving a little less selfish, and helps us to grasp our common life in the family of God where the good of one is occasion for the rejoicing of all. Correspondingly we can regret for Christ's sake something for which we appear to have little or no personal responsibility; in this regard, our common involvement in the sin of the world becomes clearer and our gratitude to God that he loves us in spite of all these evil things grows greater.

6. From thanksgiving and penitence, it is a natural move to intercession or praying for other people, and for the coming of Christ's Kingdom. Clergymen and, to a lesser extent perhaps, readers are likely to be told after a service about some relative of a worshipper who is in need of prayer for some special reason. If the reader is involved in pastoral work such as sick visiting or leading the youth club, and is not just taking services and preaching, his work is not complete unless it forms the matter of part of his intercession. Indeed the reader should be in a position to help others to pray better, and to share his own experience in prayer with others. It is as part of this sharing of experience that these thoughts on intercession are given. Three methods can be distinguished, differing in intensity, and their use depends to some extent on the knowledge we have of the person or cause for which we are trying to pray. For simplicity they can be described as intercession by intention, by extension and by presentation.

First and most easily described is Intercession by Intention. This is what commonly happens when at the time of the prayer for the Church in a Communion Service, the minister asks our prayers for various people and causes. He gives a number of biddings which probably vary from week to week, and then says the prayer which is the same each week. The biddings may be about people and places and causes about which we are already familiar; this is a help to the average worshipper. On the other hand, if the parish uses the Anglican Cycle of Prayer, we may find ourselves being asked to pray for the diocese of Athabasca or Tuam or San Joaquin and our knowledge of geography may be strained; this is followed up by a bidding for a parish or diocese about which we know nothing, and the names of three sick persons of whom we have never heard before. As soon as the list of biddings has been completed, the same prayer is said and we have little time to insert thoughts about the named persons and places even with our limited knowledge. This does not in any way invalidate the prayer. We are naming a number of people and causes before God, and then we say a prayer on their behalf. We can do this with very many kinds of prayer. For example, the Lord's Prayer can be said in this way on behalf of several people, one of whom is specially in need of God's grace for conversion, another is specially in need of God's grace because he is sick or dying, another has a new job, another is starting his training for ordination, another has just become a father. For all of them we say 'Thy will be done'; for them as for ourselves we say 'Give us this day our daily bread'. This kind of prayer by intention is valuable when we go to Communion and pray that all the benefits of the Passion of Christ may be brought to bear on behalf of the person or cause for which we are concerned and which we name before God. It can also form a legitimate part of our private prayer, and is the only way if our Intercession List is to extend beyond a very limited range of persons we know well.

In the second place comes Intercession by Extension; this takes a little more effort and calls for greater knowledge and concentration on our part. The word extension is used because on the one hand we reach out to God and on the other hand we reach out to the person for whom we pray. We stand as it were in the middle and, reaching out to God and the person for whom we are praying, seek to bring them together. Of course God knows all about the person and his needs; he knows all our necessities before we ask, in any case, but Jesus did not tell us to ignore prayer on that account and God does accept and use this kind of prayer. First we reach out to God in our minds, considering his greatness and power, his love and his willingness to heal or forgive or strengthen against temptation or whatever is the need we most clearly see. Then we stretch out to the person for whom we pray, and picture him in his particular need; the clearer the picture, the more we can put into the prayer. We then do what the friends of Lazarus did and say to our Lord, 'He whom thou lovest is sick' (or whatever the need is). As we leave the rest to God, we may find it helpful to say 'Lord, I believe; help thou mine unbelief'. This kind of mediation, standing in the middle between man and God as a link not as a barrier, is a form of prayer which increases our own concern. How it 'works' we may not know, but the more we use this form of prayer the more sure we shall be of the power of prayer.

The third form of intercession, the secret of which the reader may wish to share with others, can be described as Intercession by Presentation. It is a development of the second method, but it requires much more concentration and rather more knowledge of the person or need for which we pray. We start in the same way as before thinking about the power and love of God, and about the need of the person for whom we pray. But at this point instead of 'mediating' or standing between them as a link, we try to bring them together in our prayer. We are less like the messengers who brought the news of Lazarus' illness, and more like the men who carried the palsied man and broke up the roof and lowered him into the presence of Jesus. We picture what would happen if the person for whom we pray became aware of the presence of the Risen Christ. We picture Christ by the bedside of the weak or dying, in the house of the couple who quarrel and are bitter, in the place of temptation where we are helpless to follow, and we picture the person for whom we pray being aware of his strength and words of comfort or rebuke, of caution or of hope. He can humble pride and calm bitterness with gentleness. Our prayer can bring his love and patience and strength to bear where we would not be let in, and where we could not help even if we were. No door can keep him out, and this kind of prayer can be used to let him in.

When the reader has learned to use this kind of intercession and knows its power, he will want to share his experience with those people in the parish where he serves who want help in their prayers.

7. Prayer is not all asking nor is all the activity on our side. There needs to be a time when we are more passive and think and allow God to influence us in his way. Bible study may help us to think about God, it may lead to meditation; but Bible study is not itself meditation. The aim of meditation is not exposition but vision, thinking about God and his love and activity and will in such a way that it leads to faith and obedience. Once again there are three ways of doing this which the reader, having experienced, will be glad to share with those to whom he is trying to make God more real.

The first is what Dom Robert Petitpierre lightheartedly calls 'spiritual sunbathing', basking in the sunshine of God. To do this we turn our attention to some thought about God and just revel in it; when our mind begins to wander (as it will) we use some phrase to bring our minds back to the original thought. The effect is not unlike a cloud passing between us and the sun as we bask on the sea-shore; for a moment we are cold and then it moves on and we feel the warmth of the sunshine again. To take a particular example, suppose we use the first verse of Psalm 23 as the basis of thinking, 'The Lord is my Shepherd, I shall not want'. This does not call for detailed exposition; it is a declaration of assurance. In our thinking, we make it our own act of faith. We think about Jesus who said, 'I am the Good Shepherd'. We let the thought quietly sink into our mind and rejoice in it. As soon as our thoughts begin to wander and especially if we begin to consider the anxieties of to-morrow, we repeat the original verse to ourselves again and again. It may be said that this does not get us anywhere. No more does sunbathing, but we return from it greatly refreshed and invigorated. There is not much activity involved on our side, but we receive something. God impresses a truth on the mind in the same sort of way as the sunshine changes the colour of the skin.

Then there is a second recognisable method of meditation in which we engage in a kind of spiritual treasure hunt. In a treasure hunt we start off with a clue which tells us where to go next and then we should find the next clue; having found the second clue and being satisfied that it is genuine, the process is repeated. When using this method of meditation, we start with some thought which may well come from a verse in the Bible; this initial thought should have been chosen in advance. We think about it and a new thought is suggested. At this point we look at the connection between the two thoughts, and consider just how one led to the other. We then move on to think about the second theme and the process is repeated by which a third thought arises and so on. It is important to look at the connection between the various thoughts, otherwise the exercise can degenerate into a time of merely wandering thoughts. By means of this method of meditation, God can lead us from some truth declared by Jesus Christ to some action or change of plan in the immediate future. Alternatively the initial object of our thinking may be something very much to hand, and we can be led to a fresh grasp of some spiritual truth. There are several books of prayers which have appeared in England and in America which follow this method in one form or another.

A third method of meditation, which calls for rather more concentration, is more like a game of clock-golf than a treasure hunt. In clock-golf there is one hole in the green, but it is approached from twelve different points. So in this form of meditation there is one central truth which we try to consider from several different points of view. To give an example, suppose we take as our central theme the same act of faith mentioned earlier, 'The Lord is my Shepherd, I shall not want'. We can see this through the eyes of so many people; an old person faces loneliness cheerfully because of this, a child has no fear because it is true. Others do not live as though they believed it, perhaps because they have never heard of the Good Shepherd. The original comes from the Psalms, but what did Ezekiel (Chapter 34) or Isaiah (Chapter 40) think about it, and what did it mean to our Lord? The meditation can include some considerations of how the central truth could affect our thinking, our daily work, our relations with others in general and in particular, and may issue in the making of some resolution. If we can do something practical, however small, as an immediate consequence of our meditation this will link our prayer firmly with our daily life.

8. Many Communion manuals include a section relating to self-examination, and this should find a place in the prayer life of every Christian. This is especially true of the clergyman or the reader, part of whose work is to try to point the way to others. The point is not wholly covered by the paragraph on Thanksgiving and Penitence, for the purpose of self-examination is so to look at ourselves and our actions and our motives that we can discern the things about which we should be penitent. The traditional way of using the Ten Commandments as the basis for such self-examination is not the only way; the Beatitudes can be used, the fruits of the spirit, or the characteristics of love or charity described in 1 Corinthians 13. There are many ways but one objective, which is to see our faults and those inner motives which give rise to them in a way that will move us to penitence, and to gratitude that we are loved and used by God in spite of them. It is not part of the work and office of a reader to hear Confessions or to pronounce Absolution, but it is part of his work to teach others about prayer, which includes self-examination and the expression of penitence.

9. Prayer for ourselves and our own needs comes rightly at the end of our prayers. People sometimes ask clergymen and readers whether it is right to pray for this or that for ourselves; in fact, whether we are being selfish in praying for ourselves at all.

The teaching of Jesus is clear and simple, and the Lord's Prayer includes several requests for ourselves; we ask for daily bread, for forgiveness, for guidance and protection. What does matter is that we ask for these things not for our own sake but for God's sake, in order that his will may be done on earth, for the kingdom and the power and the glory are his. We make our prayer 'through Jesus Christ our Lord' and also 'for Jesus Christ's sake'. It is for his sake that we are making our request, and this will restrain any selfishness in our prayers. A simple way to pray for ourselves is to look ahead at the day which has begun, and realise that the Risen Christ is beside us at every moment. We may have a difficult meeting in the morning, we may be tempted to lose our temper or to tell a lie to save our face, but if we realised that Christ was there we would act differently. For the sake of Jesus Christ, we ask for patience and understanding and self-control and courage to be honest, and we make possible a greater influence of Christ on our lives.

Each person will close his prayers in his own way. However much withdrawal for the purpose of concentration there may have been, prayer leads on into the life of the day. The suggestions made here form just one possible structure for daily prayer. It is not the structure but the closer walk with God that matters. The reader, as a teacher of the faith, should be able from his own experience to be able to help others to realise the presence and power of God in their prayers.

Appendix 1

READERS IN OTHER ANGLICAN PROVINCES

THE description given in Chapter 2 of the development of the office and work of a reader since 1866 referred to the situation in the Church of England; that is to say in the Provinces of Canterbury and York, and in Wales until the disestablishment of the Church in Wales. Throughout the Anglican Communion in other parts of the world there has been a similar development and, with lessening isolation of dioceses and increasing mobility of population, it is to be expected that there would be a large measure of uniformity. But there are some provinces where local conditions have given rise to a number of material differences in both principle and practice.

Anglican Churches in Europe

English churches and congregations have been established on the Continent since before the Reformation. The number of these grew to such an extent that in 1633 congregations of the Church of England in all foreign countries were placed under the jurisdiction of the Bishop of London. The Diocese of Gibraltar was founded in 1842 and took over the chaplaincies in Southern Europe and Turkey. In 1883 the Bishop of London appointed a suffragan bishop, later given the title of Bishop of Fulham, to supervise the chaplaincies in North and Central Europe.

Since 1970 the jurisdiction of North and Central Europe together with the Diocese of Gibraltar have been in the episcopal care of one bishop, the Bishop of Fulham and Gibraltar. In addition there is a Bishop of the Episcopal Church of the U.S.A., resident in Paris, who has charge of the six American Churches. The creation of a 'Diocese in Europe' is now approved in principle.

Helping the clergy to serve these churches are about 150 readers and lay assistants whose licences must be renewed annually. There are no women licensed as readers. In addition to the usual duties readers are authorised to conduct funerals; there are countries in Southern Europe where civil law requires the funeral to take place within 48 hours of death. To enable Anglicans in remote places to receive Communion, where the chaplain has the care of many churches, the bishop is experimenting with the use of a reader to administer Holy Communion from the Reserved Sacrament. Assistance to the priest at Holy Communion by a reader is common practice; special permission is required, but is never refused if requested by the Chaplain and Church Council.

The Episcopal Church in Scotland

It is significant that the office of reader was re-established in Scotland three years before the English Convocations took their action in 1866. The Canons of 1863 relate to lay readers and catechists without defining the difference between them, and a similar phrase is used in the Canons of 1929. The lay character of the office is emphasised consistently, and Canons allow for a licence to be given without permission to preach. For many years there was a tradition of lay readership in mission and country congregations where the lay reader did a great deal more than take certain services. He was the 'minister' in these congregations, visiting, evangelising, teaching, etc. This ministry had a considerable bearing on the development of mission stations throughout Scotland, before and after the turn of the last century. The growth of the parish communion tradition has tended in more recent times to limit the service of lay readers, and many of the mission stations have been closed.

A strict training and supervision is required before Admission by the bishop or, in his absence, the dean. The licence may be diocesan or parochial and the Canon states that a bishop may appoint 'to serve in his diocese or in any specified part thereof where there is no rector or priest-in-charge' men or women lay readers. Assistance where the priest is present is not limited to lay readers, nor automatically theirs by right. For instance the Canon 'Of others who may be permitted to officiate in churches' includes a section: 'A Bishop may, in view of a large number of communicants or for any good or sufficient reason, at the request of a Rector or Priest-in-Charge give permission to a layman in communion with the Scottish Church to assist at the administration of Communion'. The growing custom of lay people (not only lay readers) assisting in this way, and in the reading of the Epistle and Gospel marks a development shared in most Anglican provinces.

The Church in Wales

The regulations applying to readers in the Church in Wales were revised and approved in 1978, and a new form of licence approved for use throughout the Province. A reader, however, is licensed to exercise his office within a particular diocese. If he moves to another diocese, his licence must be returned to the Registrar, and he must apply for a licence in his new diocese if he wishes to continue to exercise his office. Women are admitted to the office of reader and there is no distinction between them and male readers in the terms of the licence. Among other duties, a reader is authorised to read the Ministry of the Word (with the exception of the Absolution) and to preach at the Holy Eucharist; but the licence states that a reader may not administer Public Baptism or conduct the Burial Service, nor officiate or preach in a place of worship of another denomination without the written permission of the bishop.

Readers are not automatically authorised to administer the chalice, but are subject to the same regulations as other lay people to whom permission is given by the bishop by a licence which is renewable annually. While no statistics are available about the number of bilingual readers, there is no doubt that they help to maintain services in Welsh in the Welsh-speaking areas of the Province.

The Church of Ireland

Although a request was made by the Dublin Diocesan Synod in 1882 that the General Synod should consider how the services of the laity could be used in the spiritual ministrations and work of the Church, it was not until 1947 that the General Synod of the Church of Ireland approved of 'the use and commissioning of readers by the bishops of the Church of Ireland'. The Regulations distinguish between parochial readers, under the control and direction of the incumbent of the parish to which he is commissioned, and Diocesan readers who are under the control and direction of the bishop, for work in the diocese at large. A Bill passed at the General Synod in 1970 clearly defines the extent and limits of the duties of a reader. Men and women are equally eligible to be admitted and licensed as readers. Permission to administer the chalice (but not the bread) at Holy Communion may be given by the bishop to a person, admitted by the Bishop of the Diocese to the office of reader in the Church; this can be for a particular occasion or for a limited period only, when specially authorised in writing by the bishop, who may at any time withdraw any authorisation given. A licensed reader may read the Epistle, but not the Gospel, at Holy Communion. To assist in maintaining a common standard throughout the Church of Ireland, a course of training before admission, to be used in all dioceses, was approved by the House of Bishops in 1979.

The Episcopal Church in the United States of America

The Episcopal Church was for a long time hesitant to give permission to laymen to share in the conduct of public worship. There has been, and still is, an element of grading among lay readers; this is evidenced, for example, in Canon 25, Section 4, last paragraph, which reads 'He shall not deliver sermons or addresses of his own composition unless, after instruction and examination, he be specially licensed thereto by the Bishop'. Permission for a lay reader to administer the cup at Holy Communion was not given until 1964, though the subject had been raised at General Convocation many times. One of the reasons for assistance being granted was the existence of perpetual deacons, which varied greatly in number from diocese to diocese. Canon 25, Section 5, now provides for a lay reader to deliver the cup at Holy Communion, provided he has been specially licensed thereto by the bishop. The licence to administer the chalice shall be issued for a period of time not to exceed one year. Such a licence may be given to any lay person, other than a lay reader.

In recent years the participation of the laity in public worship has increased greatly. At first, it was envisaged that lay readers should be used only in the absence of a resident priest and when a visiting priest could not be obtained. The pattern now is quite different. The Proposed Book of Common Prayer, which is in general use in the vast majority of parishes, provides for wide participation by the laity in the liturgy, not only as readers but as officiants, leaders in the Prayers of the People, etc. In all these functions, women participate as much as men.

Special provision is made in the Canons for the Presiding Bishop or his Episcopal representative to grant a lay reader's licence to a member of the Armed Forces, to meet a need arising from the limited number of Episcopal Chaplains in the Armed Forces.

The Anglican Church of Canada

The Anglican Church of Canada does not have any over-all regulations for lay readers. Each diocese makes its own provisions, and the work done by lay readers varies enormously from diocese to diocese. Canon 12 of the Diocese of Toronto describes lay readers as a minor order; they shall be admitted to the order by the Bishop or by some other minister appointed by him. There are some women lay readers, but there are also women who are called Bishops' Messengers whose duties and responsibilities are similar to those of licensed lay readers and more. In the diocese of Brandon, for example, Bishops' Messengers officiate at services, conduct baptisms and even on occasion solemnize matrimony. Assistance in the administration of the paten and the cup by lay persons is not restricted to lay readers; the limitation of this to the cup only was specifically removed by a resolution of the Canadian House of Bishops in 1968. In the northern and more isolated areas there are catechists, usually native Canadians, who provide a lay ministry similar to that of readers.

The Church of England in Australia

There are no regulations which cover the work of readers as a whole, and as a result arrangements vary in the different provinces and dioceses. Readers are usually, but not always, admitted by the Bishop; he can, however, authorise an incumbent of a parish to admit a reader on his behalf. The distinction between diocesan and parochial readers depends largely on the diocese concerned. In the diocese of Melbourne, for instance, diocesan readers are expected to have a university degree or some theological qualification; parochial readers are more strictly limited to working in their own parish. Laymen other than readers are encouraged to read both the Epistle and Gospel at Holy Communion. As a result of the increase in Parish Communions and the consequent decline of Evensong, readers are less used than formerly though no less in number.

Trained women workers are now regularly given permission to share in the liturgy of the church and to assist with the administration of the chalice when there are a large number of communicants and a shortage of ordained assistants and women have also in many dioceses been admitted as readers and given authority to administer the chalice, although this is apparently more common in girls' schools or at mid-week services where women form the larger part of the congregation.

Church of the Province of New Zealand

The General Synod in New Zealand revised its Canon in respect of lay readers in 1968. The new Canon IX provides for either men or women to be admitted to the office of lay reader. In the case of a parochial reader, admission is by the vicar of the parish where the lay reader is to serve, in the presence of the congregation; the parochial character of the office is made clear from the Order of Service appointed. Diocesan lay readers are admitted by the bishop or his commissary. There are two forms of licence which differ in respect of permission to preach. One licence allows lay readers to read such sermons as may be approved from time to time. The licence to 'preach and interpret' is normally granted only after the lay reader has pursued a course of reading further to his initial training. As in most Provinces, permission to administer the chalice at Holy Communion is given by the bishop to lay persons at the request of a vicar, and this permission is not restricted to lay readers. The Canon specifically states that the lay reader may read those parts of the New Zealand liturgy entitled The Preparation, The Ministry of the Word and the Intercession. In the absence of the vicar, a lay reader may officiate at the Burial of the Dead and in cases of urgency, the Public Baptism of Infants.

Church of the Province of South Africa

Since 1969 there has been a complete change in the Canon and the regulations which govern the use of Lay Ministry. Previously the Canons spoke of catechists, sub-deacons and readers. Each was a distinct office and admission was given, once only, by a bishop in the presence of the congregation. The licence of a catechist was much wider than that of a reader, but as in some native languages the same word was used as the translation of both, there was no little confusion. In general, however, the catechist was a whole-time paid servant of the Church working in a non-white parish.

The new Canon 19 speaks just of lay ministers, who may instruct and prepare candidates for Holy Baptism and Confirmation, preach and assist in the administration of Holy Communion. It adds 'Any lay person may in an emergency baptize and, at the request of the incumbent or the Archdeacon (i) conduct Divine Service (ii) bury the dead'. There is no distinction between male and female, or any racial distinction, in lay ministers. The aim of this Canon was to make it quite clear that lay ministry is a function and not an office.

In 1978 a new regulation was prepared to provide that lay persons may be appointed to administer Holy Communion from the Reserved Sacrament to the sick in hospital or at home, or to congregations in church. This has been the practice of the Roman Catholic Church in South Africa for several years. Again, this duty and privilege may be given to men and women alike.

Province of Central Africa

The Canon relating to readers and catechists makes it clear that the only difference between them is that a reader is voluntary and a catechist is a paid servant of the Church working in subordination to and by direction of the priest. There is no distinction between their duties, which include officiating at the Burial of the Dead and baptising in cases of emergency. In addition a third lay agency is described in the Canon by the simple name 'Helper', to be given by a Letter of Appointment by the Bishop to perform specified parts of the reader's or catechist's duties. Permission to assist with either chalice or paten at Holy Communion may be given to any reader, catechist or helper, and there is no distinction made between men and women. By reason of distance, readers are not always admitted by a bishop, though they must be licensed by him. In the abnormal condition prevailing in a large part of the Province, details are uncertain and practice may be ahead of theory.

Province of Tanzania

This Province was formed in 1970 and so far no regulations about lay readers have been issued. In practice, however, there are both lay readers and catechists who are always admitted and licensed by the Bishop of the Diocese; both offices are open to men and women alike, but few women have come forward. At Holy Communion, they may read the Epistle, but not the Gospel; special permission is needed for them to assist in the administration of the chalice. In the villages they may take funerals but not baptisms (except in cases of emergency). There are paid and voluntary catechists as well as paid and voluntary readers. The training is evidently thorough, involving a period of residential training given at diocesan centres for periods varying from two weeks to nine months.

Church of Uganda, Rwanda, Burundi and Boga-Zaire

The regulations in this Province are similar to those in other parts of Africa. Men and women are eligible to be admitted as lay readers. Special permission from the Bishop is required for them to read the Epistle and assist at Holy Communion. They may take funerals, but only baptise in extreme cases of emergency. There is no distinction between catechists and readers, but there are a number of full-time paid readers with different grades. The course of training lasts for three years. Lay readers are normally admitted by the bishop, but he can authorise some priest to act for him in this.

Province of Kenya

The practice of this Province regarding readers is similar to that in other parts of Africa. There are paid catechists, employed full-time; readers are voluntary. Men and women are equally eligible, though few women have come forward. They may take funerals but not public baptisms. A special licence is required for a reader to read the Epistle and assist in the administration of Holy Communion.

Province of West Africa

There appear to be few differences from English usage in the Canons or regulations governing the work of Readers. Most of the readers and catechists are African, and ability to speak the local language largely determines their usefulness. In the remote villages they are busy giving instruction; in the large towns they are not so much used.

Province of the West Indies

There is no one general rule throughout the Province regarding the admission and training of readers and catechists. Customs and regulations vary from Diocese to Diocese. Some licensed readers are engaged in a full-time ministry as catechists, especially in the remote Out Islands. All potential readers in Guyana are subjected to a full period of training, part of which is residential, before they are licensed. The offices of reader and catechist are open equally to men and women.

Diocese of Hong Kong

In the Chinese parishes, permission is given to a layman to perform such duties as reading the Epistle (but not the Gospel) and administering the chalice at Holy Communion, or conducting Morning and Evening Prayer. The Diocese makes use of auxiliary clergy (under Canon XIXa of its Constitution) which reduces the need and the opportunities for service of readers. In the English Churches, use is made of readers who have been admitted and licensed elsewhere, who come to Hong Kong; most local candidates follow the course of training arranged by the Readers' Committee in London. On completing the course and receiving the Central Readers' Certificate, they are admitted and licensed by the Bishop in the Cathedral.

The Church in Japan

The Canon of the Nippon Sei Ko Kai relating to lay readers states 'On the recommendation of the Rector and a majority of the vestry and approval of the Standing Committee, the Diocesan Bishop may license a male adult active communicant in good standing as a Lay Reader to assist in the service and instruct enquirers under the supervision of the Rector. The licence shall be valid for one year and may be renewed'.

There are about 65 readers in the Church in Japan, of which one third are in the Diocese of Hokkaido. On the other hand, a catechist is defined as an assistant church worker with a salary, appointed by the bishop. All candidates for ordination spend some time as a catechist.

Appendix 2

EVANGELISTS AND LOCAL PREACHERS

1. Church army captains and sisters are evangelists and not readers. The office of evangelist was officially recognised by the Convocations in 1898. This was not done specifically to meet the particular needs of the Church Army, but rather to provide regulations for what was happening in the Diocese of Lichfield. In that Diocese the Bishop had set up a group of lay evangelists and, at the request of the Upper House of Canterbury, a Report was presented on the subject.

The Convocation Resolution provided that the Bishop of the Diocese in which the training house is situated should admit the lay evangelist and give him Letters of Admission to his office. In addition 'it is expedient . . . that the Bishop of the Diocese (where the evangelist is to serve) should grant him a reader's licence'. The training for the office of lay evangelist was recognised as meeting all the requirements for the office of reader. In practice, both then and now the training covered a great deal more ground and is much nearer to that of the clergy than to that of readers. The Church Army Training College, which later moved to Blackheath, was then in the Diocese of London and the Bishop of London was responsible for admitting Church Army Officers as lay evangelists. This responsibility passed to the Archbishop of Canterbury in 1963.

The present training of Church Army Officers covers three years at the Residential College in Blackheath. The syllabus is intentionally and heavily weighted on the study of the Bible on the one hand, and of modern society and methods of communication on the other. In addition, about one third of the course is taken up with Field Training under careful supervision. The whole programme of training is designed, not to train a person to conduct church services and to preach, but to be an evangelist working partly within but largely outside the parochial strucctures. The present wording on the Letters of Admission given by the Archbishop begins 'The main function of an evangelist is to help people to accept Jesus Christ as their Saviour and Lord'. The duties named in the document are similar to those named in a reader's licence, but there is little comparison in practice. About one-third of Church Army evangelists are parish workers. The majority are to be found engaged in running homes and hostels, youth centres and forces welfare centres. Some assist prison chaplains; some are engaged it itinerant mission work or with the training of laity within a Diocese. All have received a residential training, formerly two years but now three years, and are giving their whole lives as full-time paid workers.

In 1952 the Central Readers' Board resolved that the Church Army and the Reader Movement should be recognised as separate institutions within the Church of England. 'Any suggestion that commissioning in the Church Army should qualify automatically for admission to the office of reader, or that Church Army evangelists in order to function regularly in a diocese must be admitted to the Office of Reader should be resisted as both undesirable and impracticable.' Both institutions gain by this clear distinction.

Legislation in the Church of England tends to be concerned with parochial structure and the Convocation resolutions relating to permissions to be given to lay persons to take particular part in church services began by referring to readers. Thus the first resolutions about assisting at the administration at Holy Communion referred to readers; now it has been extended to other laymen. Church Army Captains frequently share this privilege. Now that this has been extended to women, Church Army Sister-Evangelists can share this privilege. In either case it is at the Bishop's dicretion. When the words 'except at the Holy Communion' were removed from the Licence given to a reader describing when he might preach, the Archbishop ruled that they should also be deleted from an Evangelist's Letters of Admission. The two offices are quite distinct, and the two institutions entirely separate, but rules applying to one have much bearing on the other. The primary distinction is that readers are unpaid and fulfil their office in their spare time; the Church Army officer is a full-time paid evangelist. There are, in England, some 350 such officers of whom one-third are Sisters. There are, in addition just over 200 retired Officers, many of whom are still working voluntarily. In addition there are 'autonymous daughter societies' in Canada, U.S.A., Australia, New Zealand, East Africa and the West Indies.

2. THE CHURCH OF SOUTH INDIA was inaugurated in 1947 by the union of a number of churches, including four dioceses of the Church of India, Burma and Ceylon. The Methodist Church in South India was another participating church. It is understandable that some of the regulations are different. The lay preacher, who has a thorough training before his examination, is admitted in a public service by the bishop. He is given a licence to preach only in the Pastorate in which he serves. Women are eligible equally with men, though it appears that the number of women serving as lay preachers is very small. The number of lay preachers altogether is large, there being approximately 250 in the Diocese of Madras alone. There is a small, and diminishing, number of whole-time paid catechists in charge of village congregations.

Lay men and women are invited to read the Old Testament and Epistle at Holy Communion, apart from being lay preachers. The bishop can license lay persons (men or women) to assist in the administration of Holy Communion; this he does in a brief public service in church. Such helpers, not being lay preachers, are known as lay readers. These details apply in the Diocese of Madras and the bishop writes that they are probably typical of most dioceses.

The C.S.I. Synod Ministerial Committee issued a Report on the Diaconate at the Eleventh Synod in January 1968. From this it appears that there are some two dozen 'honorary deacons', mostly in secular work; most appear to be hoping to be ordained to the priesthood. The Synod is engaged in re-thinking the role of the deacon and of Church as a servant community. Resolutions passed in 1968 envisage a body of men for the diaconate to become full-time, paid, permanent deacons; the C.S.I. is currently in the process of recognising women as deacons also. As the whole subject, however, is still under active discussion it is not possible to see how such development will work out; but it does not appear likely that it will in any way affect the work of lay preachers who play a quite essential role in the life of the Church of South India.

3. METHODIST LOCAL PREACHERS. The Methodist Church gives such provision to Local Preachers and depends for the maintenance of its services so greatly upon them, that a brief note indicating similarities and differences compared with the Church of England is here added. The number of Local Preachers greatly exceeds the number of ordained ministers.

The preparation and training of a Local Preacher is explained in detail in Standing Orders 575 and 576. He is called a 'Local' Preacher to distinguish him from an 'itinerant' preacher who is ordained. Indeed, length of service in the ordained ministry is measured by the number of years the minister has 'travelled' (e.g. Standing Order 720). Only in special circumstances can a candidate for Local Preacher assist outside the limits of the circuit where he is a member. He serves not less than three months on a Note from the Superintendent Minister. He is then questioned by the Superintendent at the Circuit Local Preachers Meeting as to his knowledge of the faith; he has to give an account of his conversion to God, his present Christian experience and his call to preach. During the preceding three months, he will have conducted a trial service in the presence of a Minister or a fully accredited Local

Preacher, who presents a Report of the Service to the Local Preachers Meeting. If the candidate passes this, he may be accepted as a 'Local Preacher on Trial'; the period of Trial may not be less than twelve months and normally is two years. During the whole period when he is on Note or on Trial, he comes under the guidance of a Tutor who will have been appointed by the Local Preachers Meeting; each quarter he conducts a Trial Service at which at least one Local Preacher must be present. There are also written examinations to be taken, in which stress is laid on accurate knowledge of the Bible. (G.C.E. Divinity examination at Advanced Level provides exemption from the Bible papers, if the syllabus is judged sufficiently comprehensive. In addition, the Religious Education Courses at some Colleges of Education, and some University degrees in Theology, if deemed sufficiently biblical, are accepted.) The Local Preachers' Meeting decides in the light of the examination results and the reports of the trial Services whether the candidate shall be recommended for admission as a fully accredited Local Preacher. This recommendation must be approved by the Circuit Meeting. A letter signed by the President of the Conference is delivered to each Local Preacher being admitted at a 'Recognition' Service in which the Local Preacher is received into the Order.

Local Preachers, once accredited, take their place in the Quarterly Circuit Plan and become members of the Local Preachers Meeting. Women are eligible to become Local Preacher on the same conditions as men, and when accredited enjoy all the same rights, privileges and responsibilities.

In addition to the office of Local Preacher, the Methodist Church used to appoint a number of Lay Pastors, but this order has now been discontinued.

Again, when it was considered that the number of ordained Ministers was so small in proportion to the size of the Circuit that some or any of its churches were deprived of reasonably frequent and regular administration of the Sacraments, application could be made (through the District Synod) to Conference for a suitable lay person to be given special permission to administer the Holy Communion. This is still possible in theory, but in practice is very rare indeed. (In the North West Lancashire District, for example, no such dispensation has been given during the last thirty years.)

In addition to Local Preachers, however, the Methodist Church makes use of and relies upon Class Leaders for the maintenance of its local life. Every member of the Methodist Church is supposed to have his name entered on a Class-book, is placed under the pastoral care of a Class Leader and given a quarterly ticket of Membership. The Class Leaders, together with Ministers and Society Stewards and a few other officials, make up the Pastoral Sub-Committee (S.O. 822) which is the local pastoral and disciplinary unit. Theoretically the Class Leader should call together his Class weekly, but in practice it is much more seldom. He exercises a general pastoral oversight of the Class, visiting the sick and the lapsed and keeping the Minister informed of any special need. Only those who recognise and are willing to share this pastoral responsibility may be appointed as Class Leaders or Assistant Leaders.

Thus the Methodist Church is structured in a way which makes its use of laymen and women in its pastoral care and witness part of its essential life. The working out in practice of this ministry of the laity is an outward expression of the doctrine of the Church accepted by the Methodist Church.